REALLY PROFESSIONAL INTERNET PERSON

JENN McALLISTER

REALLY PROFESSIONAL INTERNET PERSON

JENN McALLISTER

SCHOLASTIC INC.

To the woman who pushed me out of her and continues to push me forward through life—thank you for your endless amounts of love and support throughout every single one of my personal endeavors.

Very special thank you to my co-writer, Nora Kletter, for providing countless cost-free therapy sessions and for working hours on end with me to help create this book.

INTRODUCTION

Hey, person I can't see, I'm Jenn McAllister. I'm used to talking to people I can't see, because I've been making and posting videos on YouTube for almost seven years under the username Jennxpenn. In other words, I'm pretty much a really professional Internet person. If you've watched some of my videos you probably already know a lot about me. Like that the title of this book is my sarcastic Twitter bio or how I came up with my username for my YouTube channel, which I created on January 15, 2009. I wanted my username to be Jennpenn because my name is Jenn (obviously) and at the time my friend called me "Penn," but that was already taken, so I put an *x* in the middle. I think Jennxpenn sounds catchier than Jennpenn anyway. You may also know I won't hesitate to prank call my own mother and tell her that I'm pregnant or I got arrested. Or that I once held the world record for most alternate-hand selfies. Also, I hate the word *selfie*.

So much of my life is on the Internet: what I like, what I don't like, what I look like, who my friends are, where I'm from. But so much of it isn't. Even if you've watched every single one of my videos, there's still a lot of stuff you don't know about me. For example, I bet you didn't know I developed a paralyzing fear of butterflies after watching the episode of *SpongeBob SquarePants* where Wormy turns into a butterfly. That close-up scene when he lands on the glass is engraved into my brain. Or, on a more serious note, I bet you didn't know I used to suffer from extreme anxiety and often had panic attacks. There's a reason you don't know that stuff about me: I didn't want you to.

Even though I post weekly videos of myself on the Internet, I've always been a pretty private person. When I first started posting videos, I didn't want to tell anyone how old I was or my last name, basically because I believed everyone on the Internet was a creepy dude with pizza sauce on his sweatpants living in his mother's basement. Obviously, I've learned since then that's not true. So, for the record, I'm nineteen and my last name is McAllister (in case you didn't read the first sentence of this book). When I got my first PO box, I picked a post office in New Jersey—even though I lived in a town called Holland in Bucks County, Pennsylvania—so people wouldn't try to figure out where I lived (also because it was cheaper). But there were reasons beyond a fear of stalkers and weirdos that I didn't reveal a lot of things about who I am; I wanted to put on the facade that I was perfect or, at the very least, normal.

I am aggressively not perfect. I fall down the stairs an inordinate amount. I say the word *coffee* like it has a *w* in it. And when I don't have the energy to clean my room, I'll just shove everything into the corner so it doesn't show up on camera when I make my videos. Perfectionism is something I've always struggled with. Like writing this book, for example. While I was writing this book, I had this notion that whatever I wrote had to be exactly right because it was going to be published, and therefore, short of the apocalypse or some sort of *1984* book-burning situation, it's always going to be there. I spent forever reading sentences over and over again until my eyes turned red and I had a pounding headache. I was the same way in school; I was so nervous about turning in papers because I always felt like there was more I could be doing. With my videos, I'm never really "done." I always try to add more to them until eventually I decide I have to stop working on them. But if I kept working on this book until it was "perfect" I would be working on it forever, because perfection is not really a thing.

When I first started getting sucked into the Internet, I read a quote somewhere that went, "Never tell anyone your problems. Twenty percent don't care and the other eighty percent are glad you have them." I went through life with the mind-set that if I talked about certain things, people either wouldn't care or would use them to try to tear me down. I know now that's just sort of an awful way to live. It's good to talk about our faults, our fears, our weaknesses, and our experiences with our close friends for a lot of reasons. For one thing, talking about things takes away their power. When you can say out loud, "You know what, I am not a great dancer, but that's okay," it makes it a whole lot easier to attempt to twerk to Beyoncé at a school dance. But for me, the most important reason to talk about these things is that someone might be going through exactly what I've been through.

This book is full of the things you don't know about me. These are the stories about the times I didn't feel normal, the stories I wanted to forget. But they are also the stories of how I became the person

I am today, how I get to live my dreams and do what I love every single day—make YouTube videos for all you beautiful people—and more. I wanted to write this book because I wanted you guys to know that I believe in you, even if you don't feel like anyone else does. I am living proof that if you're passionate about something and you have faith in yourself, there is literally nothing you can't do. If you know what you want and work hard at it, no one can stop you. Not even that asshole in your class who shoots spitballs at the back of your head. Not even him.

Love,

Jenn

P.S.

Except for YouTubers and my two best friends from home (Hi, Jordyn and Gabriela!), I have changed all of the names of the people mentioned in this book to protect the guilty. Partly because I didn't want to give these people the satisfaction of seeing their names in print, but also because hopefully they aren't harassing anyone anymore. I have changed, and it's possible they have, too. Just like I don't want anyone to tell me who I am, I didn't want to tell them who they are. The people in this book are characters in my story; I wouldn't want to tell their story for them.

OFF-CAMERA SHY

When I was in fourth grade, I found my parents' video camera in a chest under the piano. It wasn't a fancy camera, just one of those old-school camcorders that used tapes. Still, I became obsessed with it. Making videos was an instant hobby. It's a good thing YouTube didn't exist back then. I would have had exactly two subscribers, and they both would've been my parents. Through the camera lens, anything looked interesting to me. Seriously: any random thing. I would literally go outside and film trees. Not like a nature special where you learn a lot about interesting species of trees. Just trees. Standing there. Being tall. I was so proud of my tree videos that I often turned my living room into a movie theater, making my parents watch them instead of their normal television shows. I made movie tickets out of construction paper and everything. The most tragic part of all of this is that I didn't even know how to edit yet, so I'd just connect the camera directly to the TV and play through all the footage.

When I was done filming every tree within walking distance of my house, I started making videos that actually had a point (eh . . . debatable), starting off with my own version of an episode of *MTV Cribs*, a show where celebrities gave tours of their crazy-awesome mansions. Except my house didn't have a bowling alley in the basement or an eighty-three-car garage full of Bentleys. My house was just a normal house. Still, I made a friend film me giving a tour of every room. The video was an hour long and exactly as cool as it sounds. My super-supportive parents watched the entire hour-long crib tour, which must have been particularly boring for them because, obviously, they'd seen it. It was their house.

On a recent trip back home, I found the tape I used to record all my super-old footage and of course I decided to watch it. Since I just used one tape and recorded over it again and again, the tape would just stop in the middle of a video and go on to the next one—like watching a clip show from my most embarrassing videos ever. But I did get the chance to rewatch one of my first sketches. In the sketch, my friend Penny went to visit her aunt who had a really big butt that kept knocking things over. That was it. That was the whole point of the sketch. I played Penny's aunt and we built the big butt by tying an exercise ball to my pants with a blanket. We thought it was the funniest thing in the world. I remember proudly presenting the sketch to my parents like, "This is my Big Butt Sketch."

Watching a young me swing her oversized butt into lamps, I was struck by how confident I seemed. The truth is, I wasn't. I had always been sort of a shy kid. I mean, I wasn't, like, the girl who eats her hair or the weirdo who won't respond when you ask her a question; I was more the nervous oh-god-I-hope-the-teacher-doesn't-call-on-me-wouldn't-it-be-great-if-I-could-blend-into-the-furniture kind of shy. But I was never nervous on camera. Never. For me, filming stuff never made me nervous because I didn't have to worry about doing something wrong. If I messed up, I could reshoot it.

In film, you always get a "do-over."

In life, though, I was always nervous, because you don't really get a do-over. Whatever mistakes you make kind of stick. There have been many times in my life when I wish I had a do-over. Like this one time, when I was younger, I was using the bathroom at a bank and I forgot to lock the door, and someone walked in on me. It was traumatizing. That, I'd like to do over.

My nervousness hit its all-time high when I got to middle school. It felt like just when I got comfortable with elementary school, everything changed. It was a whole new environment. We had to switch classrooms for different subjects, there were so many books to carry, and our lockers were absurdly small. My elementary school was one of a bunch that fed into my middle school, so my class size practically quadrupled overnight. The halls were crowded with all these new people, and I felt like I didn't fit in. I wasn't, like, a weird outcast who saved my toenail clippings. I did have friends; I just never really felt "in" with the friends I was supposedly "in" with. I was a little artsier and a little nerdier than they were, but it was more than that. Suddenly, my friends were all in this big hurry to grow up, to try new stuff, and I just wasn't ready. It felt like when we hit middle school everyone was figuring out who they were and I was on a different track.

I remember this time my friends wanted to have a boy-girl sleepover. I didn't want to lie to my mom, but I *was* afraid that if I told her boys were going to be there, she wouldn't let me go. I wanted to fit in, so I lied anyway. I felt super-guilty, and in the end my mom found out about it. (Never lie to your mom.) Now, I'm not saying I would've caved in to all kinds of peer pressure to fit in. No one was asking me to drink a six-pack in his or her basement or smoke cigarettes behind the gym back then. It wasn't like some crazy scene from a movie. I just had this idea in my head that there was a time and place for things.

For me, it wasn't that time and I didn't even
know how to get to that place.

I started to develop anxiety. At the time I didn't know what was wrong with me. I didn't even know what anxiety was. I couldn't pin down "Hey, I'm anxious." Instead, I felt more like, "Hey, I'm so nervous I feel like I'm going to throw up." Then I started getting panic attacks. Again, I didn't know what panic attacks were. Just that suddenly my heart would race and I'd want to crawl out of my skin.

Sometimes I'd even have them in class. It's not like anything specific would happen to trigger the attacks. One second I'd be sitting in English class, totally fine, listening to the teacher talk about *Night* by Elie Wiesel (one of my favorite books) and, like, two seconds later the thoughts in my head would get so loud they'd drown out everything else around me. It was like I was underwater.

Did you ever play that game where you and your friends would try to talk underwater in

a pool? You'd both go under and one of you would say something and the other would have to guess what it was, except it was super-hard because it sounded all muffled? It was like that—except I was the only one underwater. Everyone else sounded muffled and I couldn't pay attention to what was going on around me. All I could hear was the sound of my heart beating and air going in and out of my lungs.

Sometimes it would feel more like my thoughts were spinning out of control. I would just start thinking about something small that might happen, and I'd start creating worst-case scenarios in my head about how it'd turn out. Like, I'd think about getting called on in class, and I'd start to worry, *What if I develop a sudden stutter even though I've never had one before? What if I try to speak and instead I throw up? What if I just spontaneously pass out in front of everyone?* Rationally, I knew I was safe. I was fine. Nothing too bad was likely to happen to me even if I mispronounced the word *supposedly* and everyone laughed. But that's the thing: Panic attacks aren't rational. And when you're in middle school, sometimes everything feels like the end of the world.

TOP **10** THINGS MIDDLE SCHOOLERS WORRY ABOUT THAT THEY SHOULDN'T

1. BODY PARTS

Something happens in middle school and everyone becomes very aware of the way everyone looks. And what's worse, they start to compare. A lot of my friends were obsessed with growing boobs. I was never a bra-stuffer. I wasn't even thinking about boobs. In fact, I was pretty sure my boobs were never coming. I was too busy thinking about knees. I hated my knees. To me, they seemed more noticeable than everyone else's, like they were popping out. I would always look at other people's knees and compare them to my own. Everyone else's knees just seemed to blend into the rest of their leg. So if you caught me staring at your legs in middle school, I wasn't checking you out. I was just thinking, *Man, those are some well-blended knees.*

2. PERIODS

Because everyone goes through puberty at different times, middle school is this weird mix of people who still look like kids and people who, you know, had boobs. I fell into the first group. While now I think it would be really great if periods didn't exist, I remember actually *wanting* to get my period just to be like everyone else. But here's the thing: You don't get to decide when you get it, so don't worry about it. And also you don't really want it. Once you get your period, you're stuck with it for a pretty long time. So quite frankly, the longer you go without it, the better.

3. BEING SEXY

Maybe because boys were starting to appear on our radar, or maybe because some of us were twelve-year-olds and some of us were twelve-year-olds with boobs (I think I've said *boobs* more in this chapter than I have ever said *boobs* in my entire life), but it seemed like all the girls in my middle school were obsessed with being sexy—or at least their version of sexy, which meant pursing their lips into duck faces and sticking out their butts and hips in photos. Let me be clear. This is not sexy. What is sexy? I'm still figuring that out. I'm only nineteen, and right now I look like one of those twelve-year-olds with boobs. But I am one hundred percent positive that duck faces have nothing to do with it.

4. EVERYONE IS TALKING ABOUT YOU

I was the kind of person who thought people were talking about me all the time. When I walked into a room, if people even *paused*, I assumed that they must have been talking about me. I was the most paranoid middle schooler ever. I would get quiet, nervous, and awkward, making what was otherwise a totally innocuous situation much, much worse. You know what? Sometimes people are talking about you. Sometimes people are thinking about you. But the other 99.9 percent of the time, you know what they are thinking about? Themselves. If you went to my middle school and thought I spent a lot of time thinking about you, I didn't. I was probably too busy thinking about my stupid bony knees.

5. GETTING DRESSED

When I was younger, I wasn't much of a shopper. That has completely changed now, but back then my parents bought all my clothes. I only wore jeans, T-shirts, and sweatshirts. But when you get to middle school, suddenly some T-shirts are cool and others aren't. If it wasn't from Abercrombie, Hollister, or Aéropostale, it was dorky. Honestly, I don't know who decides these things, because certainly no one at *Vogue* gives a shit about Hollister. The whole thing seems super-random. Don't worry about this too much. No matter what you wear, ten years later you are going to think it looks stupid. Need proof? Ask your parents to show you pictures of what they wore in middle school.

6. DOING THE RIGHT STUFF

There are no right and wrong things to like. Okay, it's wrong to like killing puppies, but provided your interests are legal and don't include killing things, everything you do is the right thing to like. When you grow up, you learn that the coolest people are the ones who do their own thing. This is a lesson I learned the hard way. Even if people make fun of you for doing something kind of weird—like, say, making YouTube videos—you'll be much happier in the end doing what you love instead of doing what everyone else thinks is cool. I know I am.

7. CRUSHES

Crushes are supposed to be fun. They make you excited to go to school. They give you and your friend something to talk about at sleepovers or in the corner of the cafeteria at lunch. But when crushes stop being fun, when they start becoming an obsession, you need to let them go. The reality is that the boy whose hair you have a weird desire to touch is not your soul mate. Most people don't meet the love of their lives at twelve or thirteen. So go do your homework. Chances are, in, like, two months there will be a new boy, and he'll have way softer hair.

8. MIDDLE SCHOOL GRADES

Obviously, school is important. And you should do your homework, study for tests, and *try* to do well. But there's no need to stress out about it. No one is going to look at your middle school grades basically ever. Not when you're applying to college. Not when you're applying for jobs. Just try your best and ask your teachers for help if you need it. That's enough.

9. GYM CLASS

You know, just in general.

10. YOU'RE THE ONLY PERSON THIS HAS EVER HAPPENED TO

There are probably a lot of ways in which you are a unique person. Thankfully, there are a lot of ways in which you are probably not. I had one friend who thought she was the only girl in the world who got pit stains. Seriously: She thought there was something medically wrong with her because she'd only ever seen pit stains on boys. At one point she even worried that her parents had lied to her and she was born part boy. Obviously, she learned later this wasn't true. Everyone gets pit stains sometimes. But thinking you are the only person something is happening to is often far worse than the thing itself. When I was having panic attacks, I thought I was literally the only person who had ever felt that way. It was the biggest relief when I found out otherwise.

But whether I was underwater or spinning out of control, either way I needed to get out of the classroom. So I would ask to go to the bathroom, take a few minutes to calm myself down, and then go back into class like nothing had happened, because—as far as anyone else knew—nothing had. At one point I was asking to go to the bathroom so much my teachers started to notice. Once, my English class was going to the library to check out books for a report. During our little field trip through the hallway, the teacher held me back and asked if I had diarrhea. Mortified, I just said, "No, I'm fine," and didn't speak for the rest of the day.

I didn't tell anyone because I didn't know how to explain how I was feeling, and thought my panic attacks were so irrational that no one could possibly understand. I felt stupid attempting to say it out loud. I thought talking about it would just make it worse and that I was the only person this had ever happened to. When I eventually found out that other people were going through exactly what I was going through (via the Internet), it was such a relief. I didn't have to be alone in it. As it turns out, middle school is a pretty anxious time for everyone. And most of the stuff people are anxious about is pretty dumb. In fact, most of this stuff could be resolved if we had, like, a global middle school assembly and talked about all the stuff we thought was only happening to us.

Some of the things I was anxious about are incredibly funny in retrospect, like my knees and the fear of vomiting in class. But some things were incredibly not funny. When you're younger, you don't really notice things about yourself that are weird until other people point them out. For me, that was being super-skinny. I was always super-skinny. I still am pretty skinny. But I never really thought about it until people at school started pointing it out. When they did, I got really self-conscious, and that's when the ridiculous knee obsession started. Then some kids decided to make it, like, a billion times worse: They started a rumor that I was anorexic.

Now, eating disorders are serious health issues, and if you have one or know someone who does, you should ask a parent or a school counselor for help. But I didn't have an eating disorder. And these kids weren't trying to look out for my health. These were just mean kids being mean. It started with comments to my face, like, "You're too skinny, go eat a cheeseburger." But, like all middle school rumors, it grew and grew and suddenly it felt like everyone around me was talking about my body behind my back.

At first I became obsessed with gaining weight. I figured if I gained a bunch of weight, I wouldn't look "too skinny," and the rumors would stop. I started binge-eating and drinking nutrition shakes, but no matter how much I ate, I was still super-skinny. It's just my metabolism. I got so worried about people thinking I was anorexic that I started to have a really weird relationship with food that's still difficult for me to explain. I became afraid to eat in front of people at school. I was afraid that if I ate too much, people would think I was overcompensating, but I was also afraid that if I didn't finish my sandwich because I wasn't super-hungry, people would use it against me. I even had this weird fear that if I choked on my food it would draw too much attention to what I was eating.

Eventually, it got so bad I was too nervous to eat in front of anyone at all. The thought of it made me so anxious I would actually get sick to my stomach, and I physically could not eat when people were watching. I would eat breakfast alone before school. I'd eat lunch alone when I got home. Of course, not eating at school made the rumors worse. My mom was concerned because I wouldn't eat when we went out to restaurants. She knew I wasn't starving myself, because I would take my meal to go and eat as soon as we got home; but she also knew something had to be wrong. It was almost like I was so afraid that people thought I had an eating disorder that I had actually developed one.

When I finally told my mom what was happening to me, things started to get better. It took me a little while, but I started to be able to eat in front of people again by the time I got to high school. But in middle school, food was a major source of social anxiety for me—because food is everywhere. It's happening all the time. You go to the mall with your friends and someone wants a pretzel. Food. You go to a sleepover and someone orders pizza. Food. When you're afraid to eat in front of people, food becomes this high-drama situation it just doesn't have to be. Realistically, no one should care how much you're eating or what you're eating, and probably in the end no one did. But because of those rumors, it felt like everyone did. The fear got so big in my head that I was nervous to have fun or go out with my friends, because just when I was having fun, you know what would show up? Food. My anxiety was crushing me. But something happened when I made videos. All the anxiety, whether it was about food or knees or periods, just sort of fell away.

Up until eighth grade, I didn't even know camera shy was a thing you could be until other people in my class started posting videos on YouTube. There was this one girl who never had any facial expressions in her videos. Her normal school voice morphed into this mousy whisper. I didn't understand. I thought maybe this was some weird character she was trying to play. Then she made a video called "Sorry for Whispering," in which she explained that she whispered because she was super-nervous about talking on video; she was camera shy. I had never been camera shy. I was, like, extremely off-camera shy, but on camera I could just be me. While it was never a conscious decision, looking back, making videos became my outlet.

MY SECOND LIFE

My parents met when they were both paramedics for the fire department. When you're a paramedic, it's a job where you kind of have to be there all the time. But the same thing is true when you're a parent, so when I was born they both went on completely different shifts so that they wouldn't have to hire a babysitter. But when I started school, it became more difficult, so they both changed their careers. My dad started his own business as a general contractor, and my mom became an EMS coordinator and taught classes in the evening. My mom's job wasn't full time, but she also did federal drug testing, which required her to travel a lot. As I got older, my mom started her own business running poker tournaments. Basically, she would bring all the chips and cards, and she'd run tournaments in restaurants in the evening, after dinner hours. For a while it felt like I barely saw her; she would drive me to school in the morning, pick me up in the afternoon, and then she was off to work. Sometimes she'd be able to stay for dinner, but for the most part, at night it was just my dad and me. Even if she was home, it's not like we'd be like one of those families who ate dinner together around the table and talked about our days like those perfect families you

see on television. Instead, we mostly ate *in front of* the television—together, but in front of the television. Since my dad was home when I was home, I spent a lot of time with him and was closer with him than I was with my mom growing up.

Besides being around more, my dad was definitely the cool parent. It seemed like my mom said no to everything. Now, looking back, I understand why my mom would say no to some of the things I asked her. Like when I asked her if I could breed my pet hamsters, or if I could drive her car to Starbucks when I was only fifteen. But at the time, some of her no's felt unfair. My dad for the most part always said yes. Not only did I feel like my dad understood me more because he said yes to almost anything I wanted to do, but I also felt like I've always been more like him. Both my dad and I are more introverted. My mom and dad would always get invited to holiday parties, and he would never want to go because he doesn't like being in situations where he doesn't know a lot of people. I was the same way when I was younger; even now I prefer to hang out with a few close friends than go to a giant party where I won't know half the people there. My dad and I also have the same dry, sarcastic sense of humor. I would say something like, "Oh, boy, I can't wait to start my homework," and my mom would actually think I was serious. Who gets excited to start homework? Likewise, if she'd do something nice for me and I'd sarcastically say, "You're the worst," she wouldn't laugh and instead she'd get offended. My mom's sense of humor isn't anywhere near sarcastic. In fact, it's pretty cheesy. Mine is really dry, hardly any cheese at all (that was a cheesy joke just for you, Mom). Beyond a dry sense of humor and a penchant for not talking to new people, my dad and I also liked the same stuff. When I was done with my homework, we would play video games or watch really nerdy shows on the Discovery Channel like *How It's Made.* (We were obsessed with weird shows like that.)

For a lot of my childhood, my parents' relationship was up and down. They'd argue a lot but, when they weren't arguing, they got along great and everything was fine. I never thought much of their arguments—everyone gets mad sometimes, and it was just something I was used to growing up. It never seemed like they'd get divorced, because whenever the word was brought up, it was shot right back down. One day the fighting just kind of stopped, and it stopped for a while. I thought this was a good thing, but it turns out that they had just hit a sticking point they couldn't get past. I guess there was nothing to fight about anymore, because they were just done. When they initially told me they were getting a divorce, I didn't believe it at all. I was completely devastated; it felt like my entire world was crumbling apart. I'm an only child and at that point none of my friends had divorced parents, so I just felt completely alone.

For the longest time I didn't tell anyone; I guess I wanted to maintain the facade that I had a perfect life for some reason. At first this was relatively easy because my dad didn't move out right away, he just slept in a different bedroom, so there was really no way for my friends to figure it out even if they came to my house. But as you can imagine, there was a lot of uncomfortable tension. And unfortunately for me, there were zero moments that suggested they would get back together even though a part of me hoped they would. I blamed my dad for ruining our family, and I became extremely resentful toward him. I barely spoke to him for a long time, and eventually all of it got too much for me to handle and I just wanted him to leave already. By the fall he moved out and to New Jersey.

Even after he moved out, I still didn't tell my friends. Instead of being like, "Hey, my dad doesn't live here anymore," I told them he was away on business trips. When you're younger you don't really have a sense of what your friends' parents do, so none of my friends were ever like, "Why is a contractor going on a business trip for a whole week?" It was so weird not having my dad in the house, but it was peaceful. Even though I was mad at him, we'd get together every weekend and do something fun. I still wanted to see him, because he's still my dad after all. We'd go to the mall, go bowling, or go to this place called Peddler's Village a little ways from our town, where they had a bunch of cool shops. The possibilities were endless! (Just kidding—it's Bucks County. You haven't heard of it? Exactly.) Whatever we ended up doing was always a lot of fun and it helped me maintain the lie because when my friends would ask if I wanted to come over, I could just tell them I was busy with my dad and they would think he was back from his business trip. After a while of this, though, I stopped wanting to see him.

Part of it was that I was a teenager and I wanted to spend time with my friends on the weekends instead, and by that point I was making more videos, so I needed more time to devote to shooting and editing. But the other part of it was that it got too hard for me emotionally, so I stopped seeing him. By the time I was on school break and I had a chance to visit him, he had moved in with a girlfriend and I didn't want to meet her. So I just never went. My dad and I stopped really talking after that. I felt like I had lost not only my family and a sense of normality in my life, but also my dad and my best friend. My mom had taken a second job when my dad moved out, so I was alone a lot.

I basically retreated into the Internet.

I know a lot of people think the Internet is a really scary place full of stalkers, trolls, and catfishers, and don't get me wrong, it totally is. But at that time, the Internet felt like my safe place, where I didn't have to think about the reality of what was happening in my life. Even before the divorce I probably spent more time online than most kids, because my parents worked a lot. Besides, the Internet offers endless opportunities to kill time.

By the time my parents got divorced, making and watching videos were my preferred ways to waste time on the Internet. My friend CoCo introduced me to YouTube in 2007, but I didn't really understand

TOP 10 WAYS TO WASTE TIME ON THE INTERNET

1. MMORPGS

Playing MMORPGs, or massively multiplayer online role-playing games, is like getting an advanced degree in time wasting. There are so many different components of the game, you could seriously spend all your time playing them and not get bored. I never got sucked into the major MMORPGs, like World of Warcraft, but I was totally obsessed with this game I found on the side of a cereal box. Be careful, though; MMORPGs are seriously addictive. I know one girl who described herself as a World of Warcraft Widow because her boyfriend preferred spending time in a virtual tavern with strangers' avatars more than going out with his real girlfriend.(Obviously, he's her ex-boyfriend now.)

2. TWITTER

Tweet. Read tweets. Retweet. Tweet. Read tweets. Retweet. It's a vicious (but amazing) cycle.

3. BUZZFEED

I watched literally every video BuzzFeed posted in one day. Seriously, I once sacrificed an entire day of my life to BuzzFeed. There was this one where they had adults trying McDonald's for the first time. It's just so funny to me that someone could actually make it to adulthood without having eaten at a McDonald's. I mean, they are everywhere. While the verdict was split on the Big Mac, everyone agreed: Those fries are *good*. And those BuzzFeed videos are good, too.

4. FACEBOOK

Facebook is the ultimate way to find out what everyone you know who you don't like enough to actually see or speak to is doing. Want to know if your friend from camp is still dating that guy with the weird facial hair? Check Facebook. Want to know if your cousin actually went to Coachella instead of just talking about it like he did last year? Check Facebook. In a way, Facebook is like the ultimate MMORPG: You get a social experience without having to, you know, change out of your sweatpants or leave the house.

5. STUMBLEUPON

I get sort of overwhelmed by museums. There's always so much to see and there is no way in the world I have time to see it all, and the crowds and recycled air sort of make me feel like I'm trapped in a giant maze. Luckily, museums have curators who organize the collections, so if I want to see a photography exhibit I can just look at that little map thingy and make my way to gallery A or whatever. StumbleUpon is sort of like a museum curator, except instead of a museum, it's the Internet; and their collection is every website ever in existence.

6. NETFLIX

Whenever I want to watch Netflix, I'll spend hours clicking a bunch of different titles looking for a new movie or TV show to check out. And then I'll give up and end up watching *Breaking Bad*, *Parks and Rec*, or *House Hunters* . . . again. HGTV is my crack. And I have an Apple TV in my bedroom but not actual cable, thankfully. *House Hunters*, this show that's really just a Realtor showing people a few houses and then at the end they decide which one they want, is on Netflix. It's not even a dramatic show, but I get overly invested and find myself saying things like, "Come on, how could you go with that ranch-style house?! You know the modern one's in a better area!"

7. PUPPY SHOPPING

When I was growing up, my mom had two Shelties (Shetland sheepdogs) named Shire and Marmic. When I was a little older and my mom's dogs died, we got a Sheltie–border collie mix from a store in the mall. You know that song "How Much Is That Doggie in the Window"? It was literally that. We were walking by a pet store, and I saw this adorable puppy in the window and fell in love. I named her Mickey; she died right before I moved to LA, but I had her for thirteen years. Since moving to LA, I've missed having a dog, so when I want to waste a solid couple of hours, I start puppy window-shopping. I'll look at animal rescue and breeder websites, or sometimes I'll just Google breeds of dogs I like and stare at the cute pictures. I'm really into blue-merle Australian shepherds these days.

8. SOUNDCLOUD

I really like music. And SoundCloud is this platform where artists can upload and post content, and users can create playlists and share them with all their friends. My friends and I all have SoundCloud accounts, and we're constantly sharing bands we like. I feel like it gives you an opportunity to discover artists you'd never have heard otherwise.

9. AIM / ICHAT

In middle school I would talk to my friends all the time through AIM (AOL Instant Messenger—for those of you who don't remember AOL, ask your grandparents; they are probably still using it for their email addresses) but when I started making friends on YouTube, I started using iChat more because it had better video. iChat basically made it possible for me to hang out with my friends who lived in different states just like I would hang out with any friend. We'd play games, we'd talk about things that happened at school, and sometimes we'd even have sleepovers where we'd leave the iChat window open all night. In some ways iChat sleepovers were better than actual sleepovers, because if you had a snoring friend you could just hit the mute button. And while I don't have iChat sleepovers anymore, I still love iChat.

10. YOUTUBE

Obviously.

it—I thought Smosh was the only channel. For those of you who don't know Smosh, they are the YouTube sketch comedy team made up of Anthony Padilla and Ian Hecox. I still remember the first video I ever watched: It was called "Spiderman, Spiderman," and in the sketch Ian suggests that he play Spider-Man and Anthony play Dr. Octopus. Ian then shoots Anthony in the face with an entire can of Silly String—you know, Spider-Man's web. Anthony responds by blowing up Ian with laser eyes. It's still pretty funny, but to an eleven-year-old it was basically the funniest thing I'd ever seen. The video is only fifty-two seconds long and that's exactly how long it took to get me hooked on YouTube. In June of 2007, Smosh became the first YouTube channel to hit 100,000 subscribers. By today's standards 100,000 may not seem like a lot, but back then it was enough to make them the most subscribed-to channel on YouTube. Today, Smosh has over 20,000,000 subscribers and counting. At first I only watched Smosh because I didn't actually know how to get to other channels. But even when I did, I was still obsessed with them. Not just because they were super-popular, but because for the first time I had found people who liked to do the same thing I did.

CoCo and I decided to make a YouTube channel together in hopes of being the girl version of Smosh. We called our channel Kikoandpenn; "Kiko" was CoCo's nickname, and "Penn" was mine (don't ask why—I don't know why). We posted our first video, called "Hehh hehh hehh . . . HEHH! (Episode 1)" in December of 2008. As you can probably tell by the title, this video really makes no sense, but I'll explain the plot to you anyway: Basically, CoCo plays a mysterious stranger who keeps messing with me while I'm sleeping. She jumps on the bed, she throws stuffed animals at me, she flies this weird bird over my head, but every time I look up she disappears. Clearly, we meant for there to be an episode two, but that just sort of never happened. We posted our second video in March of 2009; it was a sketch called "Snow Zombie," and in this one CoCo thinks she's accidentally killed me by pushing my sled down the hill. That was pretty much it. There's a twist at the end but I'll leave it up to you to search for the video to find out what it is. We posted only those two videos and basically no one watched either of them. Any views that channel has are only because I mentioned it in one of my videos years later and people went back and watched it. Kikoandpenn dissolved when CoCo decided she'd rather join a band than become the girl version of Smosh. The only reason the channel is still up is because we both forgot the password, and we literally can't take it down. I started posting videos to my own channel, Jennxpenn, just before my parents decided to split.

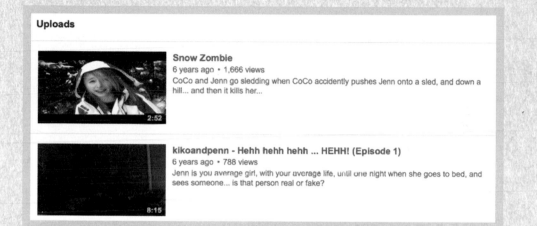

When I first started posting on my channel it was just a hobby. My first video was a stop-motion lip-dub of Katy Perry's "Hot N Cold." I made videos like that for a while until I discovered what a video blog, or vlog, was and decided to make my own that summer. My first vlog was a thrilling story about my neighbors cutting down a tree in their backyard. I filmed the whole thing and narrated each step of the tree-cutting process. Afterward I got in my dad's truck and we went through a car wash. Spoiler alert: At the end, the car was clean. Initially, it was no different from when I was filming videos for my home "movie theater." I'd have a friend over, we'd make a video, and I'd throw it up on YouTube. My parents didn't understand YouTube, they barely knew what it was, but regardless, they supported me. They checked out the videos I posted and read the comments to make sure nothing inappropriate was going on. Basically, they only had one rule: Don't talk to strangers on the Internet, because they may not be who they say they are. But when my parents got divorced, YouTube became more than a hobby, it became a way to escape my life.

It's hard to say if I was looking for a distraction, or if a distraction just kind of found me, but that summer I stumbled upon an audition for a new collab channel called FiveFreshTubers started by a YouTuber named Tyler Cleary, who was a couple of years older than me and made lip-dub videos. A collab channel is when a bunch of different YouTubers make videos for the same channel. Usually, each person is assigned a different day of the week and every week all the YouTubers post videos about the same topics. I submitted a video I made with my friend Lily called "The Chase." We filmed the whole thing with the webcam on my Macbook. There was no story. The video was just her chasing me around the backyard, jumping over tables and off walls like we were action stars. The punch line was that at the end we tripped over my dog. I was pretty sure there was no chance I was going to get in because there were so many awesome YouTubers out there, and I'm not that awesome. But I did.

When Tyler messaged me on YouTube and told me I got in, I was extremely surprised but even more excited. He asked me if I wanted to video chat with him and another girl in the collab named Micaela Romei. After all, we were going to be in a collab channel together, so we should get to know one another. Nervous that my parents were going to walk in my room and catch me talking to strangers, I joined Tyler's video chat.

I was always unsure about chatting with people I'd met on the Internet. The games I played as a kid had chat components, but I only talked to people about the games and never gave out any personal information. And you could also sort of tell when you were talking to a kid or when you were talking to someone way too old to be playing a Disney MMORPG. I had never really talked to people. But talking to people through YouTube was a totally different thing. Technically, even though Tyler and Micaela said they were teenagers, someone could be uploading some kids' videos and pretending to be them. I remember telling my friends I was going to chat with Tyler and the rest of the FiveFreshTubers, and they thought it was the weirdest thing ever. They were worried that Tyler would turn out to be some creepy old guy.

I wanted to be part of the collab channel, but I was worried if I told my parents that I was going to be video chatting with strangers, they wouldn't let me do it, so I was sort of sneaky about it. I closed the door to my room and wore headphones so they wouldn't hear anyone else's voices and would just think I was talking to my friends. I didn't want them to walk in and be like, "Whoa, who are you talking to?" I felt super-guilty about it. Of course, the second I saw Tyler and Micaela's faces I knew they really were who they said they were, and I felt less nervous about it. And once I verified that they were actually kids my age, I told my parents and they weren't too mad.

At first we'd just video chat to talk about the collab channel, but eventually Tyler, Micaela, and I just sort of became friends. Tyler lived in New York and Micaela lived in Connecticut, so it's not like we could all go to the mall together; instead we hung out through video chat. Obviously I would still hang out with my friends in real life some, but being part of a collab meant I had to post a video every week and between that and doing my homework, I was spending most of my time alone on the computer.

Maybe it was because we didn't go to the same school so there was no weird social pressure, or maybe it was because we didn't know anyone else in common, but I just didn't feel the need to keep secrets from Micaela and Tyler.

It was easier to be myself around them.

Also, Micaela was the only person I knew at the time who had divorced parents, which made it really easy to tell her and Tyler about my parents' divorce. I didn't even make a plan like, "Today I'm going to tell my YouTube friends about my parents." It just sort of came up naturally in conversation. Tyler was talking about his parents fighting, Micaela said something about her parents' divorce, and I was just like, "Oh, yeah, mine are divorced, too."

But I was still lying to my school friends. By the time I stopped seeing my dad on weekends, I had been lying to my school friends about the divorce for so long, telling them kept feeling like a bigger and bigger deal, so I started avoiding them a bit. Sometimes when they'd ask me to hang out, I would use

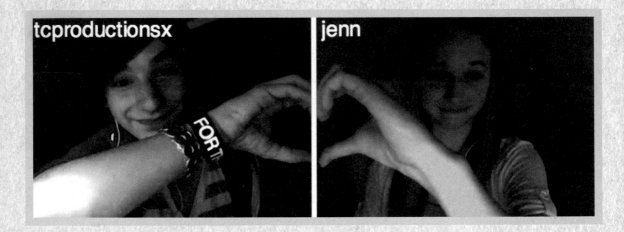

my mom as an excuse and just say she said no. Which, given how much she actually said no, was a pretty believable excuse. Instead, I would stay home and chat with Tyler and Micaela. Eventually, I did tell my school friends. One day I just sort of nonchalantly blurted out, "Oh, by the way, my parents split up," or something like that. They were super-understanding and didn't even bust me for all the lying. But by that point, I had clocked so many hours online, I started to prefer my Internet life to my real life.

My mom started to worry about me spending so much time on the computer. Even though I took my mom's side in the divorce, our fighting got worse when my dad moved out. She was worried I was isolating myself, and she wanted me to go outside and be in the real world. She didn't really get YouTube back then and didn't understand the whole Internet friends thing, so she started taking away my phone and my computer when she thought I was spending too much time inside. I was such a smartass, when she took away my phone and my computer, I'd just go on my Nintendo 3DS. On a 3DS the Internet is incredibly slow—there is totally a reason it didn't become a popular web device—but even at a dial-up pace, being able to access the Internet felt like a victory. Then my mom got smart, and she would just turn off the WiFi.

Don't get me wrong, my mom was always super-supportive of everything I did, but I had been through a lot of phases when I was younger and it was easy for her to see making YouTube videos as just another hobby. Then, one day there was this moment where it just sort of clicked for her. I've always tried to post videos on Saturdays, even before I had announced it as an official schedule. At the time, it wasn't like people were counting on me to post on Saturdays, but it was always my personal goal and I took that goal seriously. One Saturday while I was uploading my video, my mom and I got into another fight over something dumb: I'd forgotten to do some chore, or she hadn't let me go to someone's house for some reason . . . I don't really remember. But I had definitely thrown down the teenage daughter classic "You're ruining my life," and followed it with the retro but always-effective door slam. You know, super-mature stuff. Then, she turned off the WiFi. I tried to explain to her how important it was that I post that video and pleaded with her to turn it on for just a second, but she wouldn't budge. Then, I totally lost my shit. Like, I seriously freaked out. And in that moment, while I was crying and yelling and basically throwing a tantrum, she saw how important it was to me and how passionate I was about making videos.

In that moment, she saw me.

By winter I had started to crawl out of my hole, and my mom and I were in a better place. But the impact the Internet had made on my life was indelible. My mom and I are super-close now. She even got funnier. I think my sense of humor rubbed off on her. At one point after my dad moved to New Jersey, he got a new cell phone number and texted her, "Hi, I got a new number," without any explanation of who he was. He just sort of expected us to figure it out. My mom recognized the area code and texted back, "Is this my baby daddy?" My dad got so mad, but we thought it was the funniest thing ever.

Incidentally, my mom now probably understands YouTube better than, like, half of the people who make YouTube videos. She even served as an unwilling momager when I needed help figuring out what deals to take early in my career. But beyond negotiating deals like the total boss she is, she also offers me a constant source of support, strength, and love in all aspects of my life. If it's possible, I think we're closer now even though I live three thousand miles away.

 Sherri McAllister ▶ **Jenn McAllister**
January 15 ·

A note to my Daughter,
I am so proud of you and your 6 years on making video's

Jenn if I could give you one thing in life, I would give you the ability to see yourself through my eyes. Only then would you realize how special you are to me.

Remember Jenn the two most important days in your life are the day you are born & the day you find out why.

Act as if what you do makes a difference, because it does.

It's hard to beat a person who never gives up, so don't

So continue on, make your story worth telling

Love you,
MOM

Like · Comment

THAT GIRL MAKES
YOUTUBE VIDEOS

Now when I post a video on YouTube, I tweet it, post it to Facebook, maybe even post a picture on Instagram about it. But back when I first started posting, it was one big secret. I didn't want anyone to find out about my channel, because I was afraid they wouldn't like my videos or think I was weird or something like that. I only told two of my closest friends at the time, Claire and Grace, and I was even hesitant to tell them, because I was afraid of what they would think. While in my videos I seemed pretty confident and outgoing, in reality I was just that shy, nervous girl having panic attacks in English class.

It's not that I didn't want people to watch my videos; I just wanted to keep my YouTube life separate from my real life.

Luckily, at that point my YouTube life was pretty easy to keep secret; I had literally 15 subscribers and, as far as I could tell, none of them were people I knew. It was only when I joined FiveFreshTubers that people actually started watching my videos.

Tyler Cleary had around 800 subscribers, and Micaela Romei had around 200, so my audience got a little bigger overnight. Like most collab channels, each week FiveFreshTubers had a different theme. We had a music video week where we all made our own lip-dub videos to the song "3" by Britney Spears. Which, at the time, we didn't know was a song about having a threesome. We had a reverse week where we each edited clips together to be played in reverse. We even had a planking week. For those of you who don't remember planking, it's where you lie facedown in a random place. I realize this sounds totally stupid, but back then it was basically one of the most popular Internet trends. I planked on a skateboard and the roof of my house. And each week my subscriber count grew . . . very slowly. I didn't really have time to make videos for my own channel; still I gained subscribers because the collab channel would link back to mine. Through FiveFreshTubers I hit 100 subscribers (though, to be fair, 25 of those were Micaela making fake YouTube accounts to boost my numbers). I still remember it like it was yesterday. I was so excited I ran and told my

mom (who didn't really understand but was happy for me regardless), and immediately made a video with my webcam of me jumping around my room. I really wish I still had that video.

FiveFreshTubers was only ever supposed to last the summer, and when the new school year came, the channel ended like planned. Soon after, Tyler introduced me to one of his friends from Long Island, who was starting his own collab channel and wanted Tyler and me to be a part of it. That friend was Supermac18. That name may or may not mean something to you, but back then Mac Guttenberg was the biggest teenager on YouTube. He had over 300,000 subscribers, which is the equivalent of having over 7,000,000 today (I did some kind of math equation to figure that out, so hopefully it's right). And he wanted *me* to be a part of his collab channel. ME. Why me? Even today I still don't know why, but I was super-excited and definitely not going to question it. The collab channel was called MyCollab.

MyCollab was one of the first big collab channels on YouTube. We launched mid-November of 2009, when I was in eighth grade. The other people in the channel were Dalton Belew, Jonah Green, David Dalen, and Tyler, who all did mostly comedy vlogs as well, and Sundays were called "Surprise Sunday," where we would feature a surprise guest. The first week the theme was "Introduce Yourself," and my day was Thursday. I remember being super-nervous that people would be like, "Who is this girl?" when they checked out the channel, because everyone else had way more subscribers than me, especially Mac, who was bringing in pretty much all of the viewers. I literally started off my video saying, "Hey, guys, you're probably wondering who I am." In a lot of ways we weren't that different from other collab channels. We posted a lot of the same themes as FiveFreshTubers, but we also came up with a lot of new creative

David eats his own POOP (11/21/09)
7,078 views - 1 day ago

Tyler is Friday (11/20/09)
10,209 views - 2 days ago

Jenn is Thursday (11/19/09)
13,360 views - 3 days ago

Jonah is Wednesday (11/18/09)
13,135 views - 4 days ago

Dalton is Tuesday (11/17/09)
16,175 views - 5 days ago

Mac is the 1st Day of the Week (11/16/09)
16,045 views - 6 days ago

themes together. We did impressions of one another, re-created viral videos, and had a snowman-building competition when it snowed because we all lived in the Northeast. But the main difference with MyCollab was that within our first week of posting videos we were the thirty-third most-viewed channel on YouTube. MyCollab had everyone in the community talking—it inspired a lot of people to create their own collab channels, and just about every teenager with a YouTube account had auditioned to be the Surprise Sunday. It was crazy how much attention we were all getting from joining together to make videos. In just five months we had over *3,000,000* views.

MyCollab officially broke up in March 2010. A lot of rumors circulated, because the channel was kind of a big deal in the YouTube world, and no one stepped up and said why. To our subscribers it felt like one day they went to our channel and all the videos were gone. People started tweeting and posting videos asking, "What happened to MyCollab?" And since none of us were talking about it, people started a bunch of rumors.

The truth is, I don't even really know what happened. One day I was on my way home and out of nowhere I got a text from Tyler that Dalton had quit the channel. As soon as I got home I logged on iChat to ask Mac what happened and he pretty much told me Dalton had quit for no reason. But Tyler talked to Dalton, who had a different reason for why he decided to leave the channel. Mac had started MyCollab; he had the most subscribers and he was Monday on the channel, so he was often the one taking control. Maybe all of the control got to his head. He saw himself as the head of the channel, and Dalton saw it differently. He and Mac had some sort of disagreement, and he decided he was just done. Maybe he felt like Mac was making fun of his videos, maybe he was sick of Mac bossing him around, but whatever the reason, he didn't want to be a part of it anymore. When Dalton left, the rest of us had a group iChat to discuss whether or not to continue the channel without him. In the end we decided it just wouldn't be the same without him. By then most of us were also posting videos to our own channels and it just felt like it was time.

Being part of MyCollab launched my YouTube career. Not only did it get me in the habit of posting a video every week and help me improve my videos, but also, within two months of joining MyCollab I had gained 7,000 subscribers. Joining a collab channel or doing a collab video with another YouTuber is a great way to grow your channel. Most of my friends started out in collab channels like me; Ricky Dillon, Connor Franta, and Jc Caylen all had collab channels even before Our2ndLife (O2L), the incredibly popular collab, which helped make Ricky, Jc, Connor, Kian Lawley, Sam Pottorff, and Trevor Moran some of the most popular guys on YouTube. (I know O2L doesn't exist anymore, but for a majority of the stuff that happened in this book, O2L was still a thing . . . a big thing. So when I refer to O2L in later chapters, don't think I'm in total denial. Well, maybe a little.)

One of the questions I get asked most often by people starting their channels is how to get people to collab with you. I actually did a panel on collaborations called "Right Way" at Playlist Live, an annual convention where YouTube content creators get to meet their fans in sunny Orlando, Florida. The fact is, I'm still a bit reserved in real life and I prefer when people ask me to collab instead of the other way around, but I do know a lot of tips for asking someone in case you're wondering how to go about it.

In some ways MyCollab was the best thing to have ever happened to me at that point, but in other ways it was the complete worst because suddenly my YouTube life collided with my real life. I had started posting more videos to my own channel, and I was happy I was starting to stand out online, but at school I didn't want to stand out. I just wanted to fit in. I was most comfortable with people thinking of me as just,

TOP 10 TIPS FOR ASKING SOMEONE TO COLLAB

1. JOIN A COLLAB CHANNEL

When I was first starting out, I seriously stumbled upon Tyler's video calling for auditions for FiveFreshTubers. YouTube was just starting to get popular, and I didn't even know collabs were a thing. Now you can just search "collab auditions" and find tons of opportunities to join new collab channels. (I'm not kidding. I just did it. There are so many it's crazy.)

2. ASK YOUR FRIENDS

Always ask your friends to collab. You're usually hanging out anyway; why not bust out your camera? Sometimes my friends and I use collabs as excuses to hang out when we have a lot of work to do. We'll get together to film a challenge or tag and then hang out afterward, so it's like killing two birds with one stone. I find that the videos I film with friends are often the funniest because I'm super-comfortable and my friends understand my sense of humor. Think about it: If you and your friends didn't have good chemistry, you probably wouldn't be friends.

3. ASK A MUTUAL FRIEND

It's totally normal to be nervous to ask someone to film a collab. Even now, I only feel totally comfortable asking people I'm close to. Sometimes it helps to reach out to a friend you know you have in common. Friends come up to me all the time and say, "Hey, you're friends with so-and-so, right? Do you think they'd want to film a video with me?" And usually the answer is yes, because everyone in the community is always looking to make new connections.

4. MAKE NEW FRIENDS

If you're like I was and you feel like you are the only kid in a fifty-mile radius of your town who makes YouTube videos, that's okay. You can find other users on YouTube and ask them to collab. You don't necessarily need to live in the same state, or even the same country, to collab. You can each film parts of the video and send the clips to one another. Another great way to make new YouTube friends is to go to conventions specifically for YouTubers, like Playlist Live or VidCon. Talk to the person standing next to you in line at a meet-and-greet: They might be looking for someone to film with. You can even shoot a video while you're there. You know everyone at these conventions shares your interest in YouTube, otherwise they'd literally have no reason to go.

5. DON'T WORRY ABOUT SUBSCRIBER NUMBERS

When you're thinking about filming a collab, don't just ask people who have a lot more subscribers than you. There's sort of a weird sense in the YouTube community where everyone is on the YouTube ladder. It's way easier to reach out to people on your rung because it's clear it's a mutual benefit thing. If you have 100 subscribers, and your friend has 100 subscribers, they probably aren't the same 100 subscribers. Look at my first collab channel, FiveFreshTubers. None of us had a ton of subscribers starting out, but by forming a collab we all built our channels, even if only by a little bit.

6. HAVE AN IDEA IN MIND

If you are asking someone with more subscribers than you, it can be a little intimidating; at least it is for me. If you're going to ask, bring an idea. For example, in September of 2014, I had a little over 1,500,000 subscribers, and my friend Hunter March had a little over 100,000. I would have said yes to a collab with Hunter anyway, because he's a good friend of mine, but he also brought a great idea to the table that was impossible to turn down: "Pranking Guys on Tinder." For those of you who don't know, Tinder is a dating app on your phone. For the video, Hunter made a fake profile for me with a ridiculous picture and we pranked a bunch of the guys on the app for HOURS. It was so much fun to film.

7. FIGURE OUT WHAT YOU HAVE TO OFFER

Even if someone has way more subscribers than you do, you might have a skill they don't. Do you compose music? Can you teach them new lighting tricks? Can you shoot milk out of your nose on command? Whatever it is, figure out what you bring to the table. That way it makes it easy for you to say, "Hey, what if I make music for your video and you do this challenge for my video?"

8. DON'T ASK FOR TOO MUCH

I love my fans, and at VidCon I've had lots of fans ask me to be a part of their videos. One fan asked if I would be a part of her dance competition video. Now, I can't dance. I have literally no body rhythm. When I'm dancing, it seriously looks like I'm joking or something. I'm not. But I danced my butt off in that fan's video. Or attempted to. She had her camera ready; it took, like, ten seconds; it was really funny; and I was happy to do it. But I've had a lot of other fans direct message me on Twitter and ask if I will fly to their house to film a collab with them, and that's just asking a bit too much. It's not that I don't want to do it—I love meeting fans—but I just don't have time to fly out to somewhere to film a video. Also, while most of my fans are awesome and I'm sure wouldn't murder me in my sleep, there are some weirdos out there. And I probably shouldn't fly to a stranger's house.

9. JOIN A NETWORK

There are tons of YouTube networks out there, and joining a network is a really easy way to meet other people. The network will help you meet other people signed to the same network who are open to collaborating, and they'll also help organize it. I've worked with a bunch of different YouTubers through my network, AwesomenessTV.

10. JUST ASK. BUT, YOU KNOW, BE COOL.

The absolute worst thing that can happen is that someone will say no. And if they do, don't be weird about it. The chances are the reason they said no has nothing to do with you. I've had to say no to people for a bunch of different reasons that had nothing to do with them personally: They lived too far away, I had to be on stage at VidCon in ten minutes, I was going to be out of the country, I had to finish writing this book. Basically, if you asked me to collab on a video and I said no, rest assured it's not you, it's me. Unless you were super-mean to me in high school; then it's definitely you.

kind of, there. But Supermac18 stood out. People knew who he was. And since I was on his collab channel, people in my school found out about what I had been trying to keep secret. Suddenly, I went from "that girl who is just kind of there" to "that girl who makes YouTube videos."

Once one person found out, it spread around my school like wildfire. One day I was killing time on Facebook and I noticed that one of the popular girls in my school had posted one of my videos to her wall and written something like "OMG, isn't that that Jen Mackallister girl???" There was no hiding it anymore.

Jenn McAllister
August 26, 2009 ·

everybody discourges me and nobody encourages me. so what am i supposed to do? nothing? okay sure. 😑

Like · Comment · Share

Write a comment...

My secret was out. And it turns out my fears about people finding out were completely rational.

Toward the beginning of MyCollab, it started out slow—a few people making cracks about my low subscriber numbers, a couple "your videos suck" comments covered by a fake cough. Then they took to the Internet. They started posting my videos on one another's Facebook walls just to make fun of me. At that point people at my school had just started using Twitter and they would tweet screenshots with rude comments like "She's just embarrassing herself" and "Who does she think she is?" But by spring, when MyCollab ended, it got to the point where, when I walked down the hall, people would do anything to make me feel terrible about myself. They'd point at me, laugh at me, even scream my username. I couldn't get through a day of school without my YouTube being mentioned at least once.

When MyCollab ended, I was able to focus all of my energy on my own channel. In some ways this was great, because I didn't have to follow a theme every week, so it gave me a chance to get creative and come up with my own unique ideas. Even though most of the comments on my videos were positive, the shitstorm at school made it easy for me to focus on the negative. I've always been sensitive, and when I was being picked on I was super-supersensitive. I didn't want to stick out anymore, so in the middle of eighth grade I started deleting any videos that kids at my school made fun of. I'd sit at home deleting videos I spent hours on, videos I was proud of, just because people in my school made rude comments about them. I deleted so many of my videos off of YouTube and I didn't have backups of them on my computer, so I lost them forever.

To this day, it's one of my only regrets.

I think the worst part of it was that someone had actually created an account on YouTube just to make fun of my videos. The subscriber name was a play on my channel name, something like jenniferxpennifer. There are a lot of fan accounts now on YouTube, Tumblr, and Twitter with names like that, and I think it's my favorite thing in the world when my fans make those accounts, but this wasn't a fan account; this was a hate account. This account left paragraph-long comments on every single one of my videos explaining why they "sucked." And jenniferxpennifer didn't just comment on new videos I posted, they even went back to comment on older videos and left hate messages. You know, just so I was sure I knew all my videos sucked. Some of the details were oddly specific and comments were typed in a similar voice of someone I knew. I didn't have very many subscribers at the time and the attacks felt very personal in a way other negative comments didn't. Within an hour I figured out who it was, because I'm the best Internet detective ever. No, seriously, ask anyone. I can find out about anyone or find anything on the Internet faster than you can believe. I found out that the person who created jenniferxpennifer was one of my close friends. I didn't want to believe that someone I trusted would do this to me, but when I confronted her she immediately confessed. The creator of the hate account was my friend Grace. And to make it just a little bit worse, she confessed she didn't do it alone; Claire helped her. Literally the only two people I had trusted with my secret, because I was afraid of what people would think at school, created a hate account to tear me down.

THUMBS-DOWN

I hate the word *bully*. To me it seems like a silly, almost cute word that you could use when talking to, like, a puppy or baby. "Aw, look at the little bully." And people who are bullies are aggressively not cute. But I also hate the word *bully* because the definition implies that their victims are somehow smaller or weaker. While physically that may be true (you don't see a lot of short, skinny kids shoving linebacker-sized eighth graders into their lockers), when it comes to character, to integrity, to the stuff that really matters, "bullies" are most definitely the smallest people. So I don't like to call them bullies; I prefer to use a more accurate term to describe people who make it their goal to put other people down. I call them *assholes*.

Look, I'm definitely not perfect. I try not to talk about people behind their backs, but I'm not going to pretend I've *never* gossiped. Everyone does. Someone does something unorthodox or discourteous and the shit talk just sort of starts spinning. Gossip is, like, the primary energy source for middle school and high school conversation. But once you leave school, it should stop there. It's just time to grow up. Sometimes it sort of sucks you in, and you forget that the people you are talking about are, like, actual people with actual feelings. But I can really only think of one time in school when I truly was an asshole.

When I was in third grade, our class did projects on the book *Because of Winn-Dixie*, the story of how a scraggly stray dog changes the life of a lonely ten-year-old girl. We had to make a bunch of drawings that had to do with important themes in the book. In the book the dog, Winn-Dixie, loves peanut butter. To illustrate this, one boy in my class drew a picture of Winn-Dixie licking peanut butter, only the way he drew the dog's tongue was ridiculously long. It looked like he had first drawn the dog on one side, then the jar on the other, and then realized he'd have to create a superlong tongue bridge in order to bring them together. When I saw it, I pointed at it and started laughing—like hysterically. And the thing about hysterical laughter is that it's contagious. Suddenly, everyone in the class was laughing at this drawing of a dog with a really long tongue. Well, not everyone. The boy who had drawn it was not laughing. He was crying. And it was my fault. He had put effort into his dog picture, and I had put him down.

Maybe it was because I could see its effects, but for the most part I never really understood the impulse to spread hate. Of course there are people that I don't get along with for whatever reason. But I don't really feel the need to be an asshole to anyone personally. It just seems like way too much effort for no reason. Even online, I never post hate comments on videos. If I stumble upon a video I don't like, I just stop watching the video. I don't see the point of wasting time on things I don't like. I mean, in the time it takes to leave a hate comment, I could be watching an awesome video.

Unfortunately, not all people online feel the same way.

As I gained viewers, I had to deal with a lot of random online haters. Strangers on the Internet started pointing out things about me that I didn't even realize were flaws. When you're younger it's like you don't really realize your flaws until other people point them out. You're in your own little world until someone comes along and says something that makes you snap into reality. I started hating parts of myself that people would comment on. I got really insecure about things that made me different from other people. And just like people spread rumors at school that I was anorexic, Internet strangers also made comments like "You're too skinny, eat a cheeseburger." I wanted to reply, "I eat cheeseburgers all the time," but I didn't think people would believe me, so I just sort of internalized everything.

People would pick apart literally every detail of my face, which made me super self-conscious. They made comments about the freckles on my face, which, until they were pointed out, I never really cared about. Once I got my braces off, I think I felt pretty good about my teeth; the truth is, I barely

thought about them. But people commented that they were too big for my face. And suddenly I would see my teeth in the mirror and think, *Oh my god, they're right*. Apparently, I don't have a nose; I have a beak, because some people started calling me a bird. One of the most upsetting comments was that I have a constant double chin. It gets worse when I laugh. It's not like I could lose weight just under my chin to make it go away. I tried doing chin exercises, but it turns out those aren't really a thing. There was nothing I could do to get rid of it. Trust me, I Googled it. But as hard as it was getting hate comments from strangers, the hardest thing was walking down the halls of my high school.

I was so nervous to start high school. My panic attacks had mostly stopped and I had worked through my issues with food, but I still had a lot of anxiety about what people thought about me, or what they would say to me. My high school was a large public school with a bunch of different middle schools funneling into it, and it didn't seem to matter to the kids there whether they knew me or not. Suddenly, there was a larger pool of people to scream, "You suck," at me in the hallway. Strangers in my grade, even seniors I had never seen before, all had something negative to say about me.

By ninth grade my channel had grown to over 40,000 subscribers, so instead of telling me how much my videos sucked, kids started making "famous" jokes. People would sarcastically ask for my autograph outside my locker: If I said no they'd say that I hate my fans or something equally ridiculous; but if I signed something for them they turned it into a big joke. They would say things on their Twitters like "Jenn walks around school acting like she's so famous," when nearly one hundred percent of the time I wouldn't even know the people who wrote the tweets. The only reason I even knew they went to my school was because they'd post pictures of me they took in the hallway or the cafeteria. And I'm pretty sure I didn't give off that vibe, because I tended to keep to myself at school.

At school, the torment escalated. People started passing my number around, and I started getting prank calls and texts in the middle of the night. Some people would pretend to be fans and text things like "I'm your biggest fan" and "I have a shrine to you in my closet." I knew they were people from my school, because they all had the same local area code as me. But most of the texts just said really rude things. "Your videos suck," "Why are you even trying?" "Delete your channel," even "You're worthless." My self-esteem had literally hit rock bottom. There were days when I'd stay home "sick" just to avoid people making fun of me. There were even days when I came so close to deleting my channel. I'd stare at the delete button, my finger hovering over the trackpad, my heart beating so hard I felt like it was going to jump out of my chest. I would think to myself, *You could do this; you could click this button and it would all stop. You could go back. You could be invisible; all you have to do is click delete. But I didn't. Something inside told me to just push through it.*

It helped knowing that a lot of my YouTube friends were going through the exact same thing. By then I had made friends with most of the guys from O2L, Jack Baran, and a few other YouTubers. We all watched one another's videos and generally made the same type of videos, so we started tweeting at one another to break the ice, just stupid things like "Hi" or "Cool video." Eventually, we started video chatting on iChat. We were all around the same age and had roughly the same number of subscribers, so we went through a lot of the same experiences. We didn't really talk about it in a sensitive way, more in a "Hey, some asshole said this to me at school today" way. But still, hearing their stories, even if just mentioned in passing, helped me know I wasn't alone in this.

By freshman year I thought I had found real friends. I started spending time with this girl Veronica and her friends Hailey, Teri, Chloe, and Julia. Veronica and I were definitely very different. She was totally the type of person who was ready to grow up fast, where I, you know, wasn't. And where I would rather swallow thumbtacks than speak in front of the class, Veronica was the kind of student who always raised her hand. We met in seventh grade, and by freshman year she became my best friend. I was so sure this time I had found an actual friend I could actually trust.

But I hadn't. Looking back, there were definitely signs. As far as I knew, she wasn't making fun of me, but she never really stood up for me, either. Veronica's boyfriend at the time had been part of the anorexia rumors in middle school. One time, when we were all hanging out, he made some kind of anorexic joke and I got so genuinely upset that I made some kind of excuse to leave. It bothered me that she didn't even deny the rumors and tell him to shut up, but it's kind of hard to tell your friend that her boyfriend is being a dick. I told myself, *It's okay; it's not like Veronica is saying stuff about me.* But I think after what happened with Claire and Grace I just needed to believe Veronica was for real.

Then one night at the end of sophomore year, Julia and I were hanging out on our own and she told me that Veronica had been talking shit about me behind my back. And not just about my videos, but, like, everything. She made fun of my clothes. She said my videos were stupid. She told people I thought I was "such a big deal" because I had a YouTube channel. When I went to prom with Tyler Cleary, she made fun of my dress, even though she told me I looked pretty to my face. All of that and more, and hearing the extent of it felt like a total betrayal. In that second it was like she became a totally different person to me.

I didn't confront her right away because we already had plans to go to VidCon 2012 together. After we got back from California I couldn't really take it anymore. I was a little scared to confront her in real life about all the things she had been saying about me, so instead we got into a dramatic text fight. I told her she wasn't a real friend if she was talking all that shit behind my back. At first she denied it and claimed she had never said anything about me, until finally we got to a point where she just wanted to know who told me. She didn't even really apologize; it was like she just wanted to know which one of our friends she could blame for getting her into that conversation. She didn't get that she was to blame, no matter who told me, and I was done being friends with someone who would treat me like that.

Jenn McAllister

1. IGNORE IT

I never wanted to get noticed in high school. If there were some kind of locker-print camouflage jumpsuit that could have made me invisible in the hallways, I would totally have invested in, like, fifteen of them. But some people want to be noticed, and being an asshole is a great way to do it. People who pick on others are only doing it for a reaction. If you respond to it, you're giving them exactly what they want: attention. This stands true in school hallways and online: When I posted my first videos I read all of the comments, because there weren't that many, and I'd respond to almost all of them—even the negative ones. But when I responded to people who left negative comments, they would just reply with something even worse. Internet trolls will lie, offend, and exaggerate just to get a reaction. It's like a game to them; don't play it.

Jenn McAllister

2. BLOCK IT

The block button is there for a reason. Your cell phone—or any social media app you can think of—has a block button. If ignoring people who are bothering you doesn't work, use it.

Jenn McAllister

3. CONFRONT IT

It'd be awesome if there were a block button in real life. Some switch you could flip that would polarize the air around you and repel assholes away like they were the wrong ends of a magnet. (I like science, okay?) But there isn't. Even if I could have blocked the hate account jenniferxpennifer, I couldn't ignore the fact that friends of mine were doing something that gross behind my back. I'm not really one for confrontation, but on some small level I am because I hate people being shady. It's really hard for them to stay shady if you say out loud to their faces, "Hey, I know what you did; stop it."

Jenn McAllister

4. DON'T CHOOSE IT

As much as it totally sucks, you have absolutely zero control over other people's choices. But you do have a choice in your own life; you can choose not to be friends with those people. I know when you're younger it seems like having a million friends is the most important thing ever, but the friends who are shitty and talk behind your back aren't actually your friends. They're just those terrible people you sit with at lunch. Choose quality over quantity.

Jenn McAllister

5. DON'T SEEK IT OUT

By the time I got to high school, people mostly stopped posting hate comments and links to my videos on Facebook. Don't get me wrong, this wasn't because people got nicer; they just shifted from Facebook to Twitter so they could spread the very important message that "Jenn sucks" to people outside of their direct social network. While it sounds worse, in a way they sort of unintentionally did me a favor, because their comments no longer showed up in my Facebook news feed. Sometimes people I was following would favorite and retweet stupid things people would say about my videos, and I'd catch glimpses of what was being said; for the most part, if I didn't search my name, I was fine.

Jenn McAllister

6. DON'T TAKE IT PERSONALLY

My mom always says, "If you don't know them personally, don't take it personally." I've definitely wasted a ton of tears on people who didn't deserve them. But now there are only a few people whose opinions really matter to me: my friends, my mom (sometimes I can't make a decision unless I know my mom is on board. I like us to be on the same page), and the person whose opinion matters to me most . . . me. I've been in situations where I have thought, *If this were someone else, what would I tell them to do?* And I do that thing.

Jenn McAllister

7. DON'T TAKE IT SERIOUSLY

Everyone has flaws. Your favorite celebrity, your mom, your dad, I bet even your dog has flaws. You can sit around moping about things you don't like about yourself, or you can learn to accept them. I know this is easier said than done, but I've learned that if you can laugh at your flaws, other people can't use them against you. This one time I posted a picture on Twitter of me in a pretty tight shirt at an event, and my boobs exploded Twitter. People started speculating crazy things, wondering if I got a boob job or if I was wearing a special bra or something. It definitely made me feel a little weird and uncomfortable that a bunch of strangers were talking about my boobs. "Jenn's boobs" or something like that literally became a trending topic on Twitter because so many people were talking about it. But when I looked at the questions people were asking, I couldn't help but laugh. *"Where did Jenn's boobs come from?"* Pennsylvania, like the rest of my body. *"Where has she been hiding those?"* I keep them in a secret compartment behind a hidden bookshelf in my room. *"Where did Jenn's boobs go?"* Back under the baggy sweatshirts I tend to wear every day because I'm a fashion icon. Life is way too short to be serious all the time anyway.

Jenn McAllister

8. DON'T SERVE IT BACK

You know that clichéd expression "revenge is a dish best served cold"? It means you should cool off rather than seeking vengeance in the heat of the moment. While it's not a terrible idea, here's a better one: Revenge is a dish best served never. While it may feel good for a second, maybe even a day or two, getting back at someone doesn't solve anything. Not only does it make things worse, but it makes you look just as bad as the person you're seeking revenge on.

Jenn McAllister

Jenn McAllister

9. DON'T CREATE IT

Everyone knows that being mean in person is, well, mean. But some people think being separated by a computer screen gives them the right to be assholes. Obviously, face-to-face comments are the worst, but online comments can still hurt just as much. You don't like it when people say stuff about you online, so don't do it to other people. Think before you post.

Jenn McAllister

10. KNOW IT'S NOT ABOUT YOU

Hailey would laugh when upperclassmen made jokes about me in the halls. I didn't really care, because Hailey was just kind of a filler friend that I low-key didn't like. Still, I figured she must have something against me. But the truth is, Hailey didn't hate my videos, or think posting on YouTube was stupid. In fact, a couple years later, when we weren't even pretending to be friends anymore, she came up to me in the locker room and told me that of all the kids at our school who had started YouTube channels, mine was the best and I should keep going with it. Hailey making fun of me had nothing to do with me, and everything to do with herself. It was about the fact that she was massively insecure and desperate to fit in at any cost. She thought laughing along with everyone else made her cool and would help her climb up a rung on the social ladder. Just for the record, it didn't.

Eventually, I learned to grow a thick skin. I still read comments on my videos for the first couple days to see the initial reaction, because the first comments on my videos are usually from my subscribers and other people who like my videos. If those people respond negatively to a certain video, I want to know, because I actually value their feedback. But when videos have been up for a while, the more critical comments generally come from Internet trolls or people who randomly stumbled upon them and may just not like my style, so I don't really tend to look back. My fans' opinions matter, but I'm never going to make a video that every single person on the Internet will like, simply because it's just not possible. I'm not going to say negative comments never affect me anymore—some do. The one comment I sometimes get that bugs me the most is when people say I don't put effort into my videos anymore. The reality is, I put *more* effort into my videos now than I ever really have before.

I'm now realizing I just gave you major ammo if you ever wanted to hate on me. But over the years I've learned that if you stay positive, you can make it through anything.

TWO CENTS

Have you noticed how some people love to throw in their two cents even when you haven't asked for it? Seriously, it's basically impossible to go through a day without someone trying to offer you advice. "You can't park there after six p.m." Um, thanks, it's 11:15 a.m. "You should probably stop eating those cookies; that's, like, your fifteenth one." Um, thanks, but I'm still going to eat them. I'm not saying I'm much better. While I tend to mind my own business, in this book, I've given you more than my two cents; in fact, I think I've probably thrown in more like $1.76. I apologize if I sound super-preachy. A lot of the things I've talked about are just things that have helped me out and I thought I'd share them with you guys in case they help you out, too. Believe me, I know I don't have all the answers. There are a lot of things I'm still figuring out, like, for example, how not to fall down the stairs.

Seriously, there is this one step in the middle of the staircase leading to my bedroom that I swear becomes invisible when it's dark. I don't know if it's some sort of shadow cast or the way the dark hardwood floor looks at night, but I miss it almost every time and tumble the rest of the way down. It's a miracle I've never really hurt myself. Also, when I do my wash, I take forever to put away clean clothes. I'm still figuring out how to go from step one, washing the clothes, to step three, putting the clothes away, in the same day. Also, yes, I say *wash* instead of *laundry*; I know it's weird, I've heard it from Rebecca Black a million times.

While you should definitely not *follow* all the advice everyone gives you because it may be stupid, you should always *listen.*

You never know when someone is going to say something that might actually be useful.

That's some more advice from me that you may or may not follow. My sophomore year of high school, one of my teachers gave me some advice that changed my entire life.

When word got out about my channel, my teachers were always really supportive. Some of my teachers were maybe even a little too supportive and wanted to show my videos in class. I always asked them not to, but sometimes they did it anyway. I know in my videos I don't seem self-conscious, but I am. I like when people like my videos; I make my videos hoping people will like them. I don't like when people watch my videos in front of me. I get embarrassed. I get this tunnel vision because I don't want to see the look on anyone's faces, and this wave of heat sort of takes over and I feel like I'm turning crazy-red, even when it's just in front of my friends, let alone a classroom of my peers.

One time I made a video about school, and one of my teachers decided to play it in class. In the video I talk about how I got detention for being late to school, jokingly saying, "Bitch, I show up when I want." Right as that part of the video played, the vice principal walked by. He stopped into our class and asked my teacher to replay it. After "Bitch, I show up when I want" played aloud in the school for the second time, the vice principal said, "I gave you that detention." I remember being totally frozen in my seat, thinking, *If I just sit perfectly still, maybe I can make myself invisible.* Thankfully, nothing really happened, but it was super-embarrassing.

I never really got mad at teachers who showed my videos in front of the class because I know they were just doing it because they were proud of me. I had the same teacher for Honors English in both ninth grade and eleventh grade, and she always told me how proud she was to see my growth over those three years. Junior year, my AP World History teacher wrote "xpenn" after my name on an exam blue book and drew a heart next to it. I'm super-grateful to all the teachers who supported me through a time when being a YouTuber in school was not always the easiest, but the teacher who had the most impact was Mr. Hentz, my history teacher sophomore year.

Mr. Hentz was a great teacher who always seemed genuinely excited to be teaching our class. I tend to connect with teachers who are passionate, and my favorite subject would change based on the teacher who showed that the most. Because of Mr. Hentz my favorite class sophomore year was history.

TOP 10 BEST PIECES OF ADVICE I'VE EVER RECEIVED

1. TREAT PEOPLE HOW YOU'D WANT TO BE TREATED

While most of the top ten lists I make are in no particular order, this piece of advice is first on this list on purpose because it's the thing that my mom says to me the most. It's something that stems back literally as far as I can remember. Whenever I was put in a situation where I was treated badly and I could easily reciprocate the action, my mom would begin her speech, "You know what I always say . . ." She wouldn't even need to finish her sentence.

2. YOU CAN'T PLEASE EVERYBODY

This is something I've always struggled with until a recent phone call with my mom. Even if something makes most people super-happy, there's gonna be at least one person who hates that thing. As my audience grows, so does the number of opinions posted about my videos. While I hope most people are happy, I've seen a lot of comments like "I miss your old videos," and "Oh, you've changed." The truth is, I have changed. I'm not thirteen anymore; I'm nineteen, and those six years are basically the six years you change the most. I mean, imagine if I continued to pretend I was thirteen my entire life. It would be pretty weird. It wouldn't feel like me. And, even if I did it, I guarantee I would get a bunch of comments saying, "Why are you running around screaming? You're not thirteen anymore."

3. DON'T MAKE A PROMISE YOU CAN'T KEEP

When my parents got divorced, my dad made a lot of promises he didn't keep. One of the first things he said when they told me they were splitting up was, "Regardless of the fact that your mom and I are getting divorced, I will always be there for you and your mom." He then explained he meant both emotionally and financially. Didn't really happen. Later on he promised he had broken things off with his girlfriend and was going to try to patch things up with my mom. That wasn't even remotely true. He just wanted me to stop being mad at him, but getting my hopes up and dropping them flat on the ground was no way to do it. After so many broken promises, it's gotten to a point where I can't believe anything he says. Don't promise things you can't deliver, even if you think it's what people want to hear. In the end, people will be happier knowing they can trust you than they would be thinking you can follow through on a promise.

4. DON'T EAT THAT

Expiration dates on food are real. There are some things that stay good a little longer, like eggs. There is this cool test where you put eggs in a bowl of water and you can tell how fresh they are by the way they stand. If they lie flat on their side, they are super-fresh. If they stand up on one end they aren't as fresh, but they're still safe to eat. If they float, throw those suckers away. I tried it once when Andrea Russett and I were making brownies and our eggs were a little past their expiration date; I ate, like, a million of those brownies and didn't die. But generally, if it smells funny, if it's changed color, if it's no longer the same shape it was when you bought it? Don't eat that. Also, don't eat prepacked sushi from a gas station or a grocery store.

5. TAKE BREAKS

I often get really stressed out when I have a lot to do and it feels like there isn't enough time to get everything done. So I'll make a list (I LOVE lists) and I'll try to power through, but generally, overworking yourself can just make the stress even worse. So even though it sounds sort of weird to say "take breaks" when you already feel like you don't have enough time to do everything, I find that taking breaks actually makes me more productive. So grab a snack, listen to some music, or watch a YouTube video. I promise, those five minutes off will give you the energy you need to check everything off on your list. (And isn't checking things off really the best part of making lists anyway?)

6. DON'T TALK. JUST ACT. DON'T SAY. JUST SHOW. DON'T PROMISE. JUST PROVE.

Some people are all talk. They talk a big game about wanting to be a movie star or climb a mountain or run a marathon. But when it comes to actually doing that thing, they're full of excuses. It's great to have goals and it's totally fine to talk about them, just make sure you're actually doing something to achieve those goals, even if it's something small. There's never really a valid excuse for anything. You want to star in a movie? Start by taking an acting class or making a short with your friends. You want to climb a mountain? Start by taking hikes while you save up for that trip to Kilimanjaro. Want to run a marathon? Start by running a couple miles and build your way up. Even if your goal seems impossible, if it's really important to you, you'll find a way.

7. IT TAKES NOTHING TO JOIN A CROWD. IT TAKES EVERYTHING TO STAND ALONE.

Remember in school when they made you watch those videos about peer pressure where they spun out all these crazy scenarios about situations when you might be offered drugs? Then they told you these cautionary tales about kids who said yes to drugs and how they ended up homeless, in jail, or dead. Then they gave you these stupid phrases to say if someone offered you drugs, like "No, thanks—I'm high on life." In reality, it's not that hard to say no to drugs. Just say no. The peer pressure stuff that's actually hard is when you're trying to do something you love and other people are putting you down for it. "Be yourself" sounds really simple, but it's really not. Fitting in is so much simpler. But fitting in doesn't actually make you cool; it just makes you like everyone else, which is pretty boring.

8. NOT EVERYONE WHO SMILES AT YOU IS YOUR FRIEND

One day during my sophomore year I got a Facebook message from this really cute guy at my school, and for one hot second I thought, *Oh my god, he likes me.* We started texting for a bit and he mentioned that he also made videos and for two hot seconds I thought, *Oh my god, we like the same things. And he likes me.* Then suddenly he only wanted to text about videos, and I then realized he didn't like me *like me* at all; he wanted something from me. After a day or so of texting he started asking me to do things for him, like make a new outtro for his videos. *That* felt *awesome.* Some people have the wrong intentions when you're getting to know them. And some people want to see you fail just because they aren't succeeding. Which sucks, but it happens. When you're making new friends, make sure they're in it for the right reasons.

9. NOBODY'S IN CHARGE OF YOUR HAPPINESS EXCEPT YOU

When I was younger I let a lot of other people decide how I felt about myself. When people told me my channel sucked and that I was worthless, I spent a lot of time wondering if they were right. This is something my friends and I talk about a lot. You can read a hundred nice comments on a video and one mean comment, and sometimes you can only remember the mean one. It's hard to focus on the positive sometimes when the negative hits so hard. But as much as you can't let that one negative comment determine your happiness, you can't rely on those hundred positive comments, either. When I was younger I let external successes and milestones validate the way I felt about myself. But in order to be happy you can't depend on other people's positive feedback; you have to find validation from within.

10. ASK MOM

Literally, this list could just be titled "Shit My Mom Says." Most of them even came from this one letter she wrote. She's that good.

But beyond being super-passionate, he was also really aware that students have different learning styles, so he put so much time into making sure everyone understood what he was teaching. He would create PowerPoints that were dynamic and easy to understand. His written notes were always very well laid out, which made it easy for me to be crazy-organized and take obsessive notes just the way I like. He included a lot of graphs and images so visual learners could easily follow the subject matter, too. But that's not exactly how he changed my life.

It was so random. About halfway through the year, he stopped me at the end of class and asked me what I wanted to do for the rest of my life. I don't really know what prompted him to ask me, but I think it's because I had this USB drive in the shape of a camera hanging from my backpack. All my teachers knew I was into YouTube and photography. I think the questions "What do you want to do for the rest of your life?" or "What do you want to be when you grow up?" or even just "What is your plan?" can be really scary because, honestly, when you're fifteen, how the hell are you supposed to know? I feel like when you're, like, four or five, it's easy to come up with an answer because the future feels really far away. It's easy to say "I want to be a fireman" or "I want to be ballerina" or "I want to be the president" because you don't have to think about what actually goes into being any of those things. No little girl is sitting in ballet class thinking, *I don't want to be a ballerina because I'm afraid of getting premature arthritis.* But when you get to high school, and you start thinking about college, the future starts to feel like it's really close—too close.

So when Mr. Hentz asked me what I wanted to do with my life, I was super-nervous because the truth was, I didn't have a real answer.

I'd always been really concerned about my future. I grew up in a family where money was tight, so going to college and getting a stable job was my definite plan. I had expectations of what my life was "supposed to look like." I had done well in school and I had things I was interested in, but there was never anything I really wanted to be when I grew up. I only knew one thing: I didn't ever want to have to worry about money. My hometown was a pretty affluent place. Most kids weren't bothered about things like how they were going to pay for college. My family was always okay; we had a nice house—it even had a pool—but when my parents split up, suddenly money got tight. My mom had to work two jobs for a while. She tried her best to hide her money worries from me but it was always something I was very aware of. When my dad left, we stopped going out to dinner. Going shopping for fun wasn't a thing anymore. Our Christmases got dramatically smaller. Even though she never talked about bills and stuff like that, I could tell she was really stressed out. One morning she was driving me to school and she started panicking for some reason. She got so upset to the point where she even started to cry a little, and I had no idea what was going on. At the time she *just* told me she was *just* running really late. Now I know that she was running low on gas because she couldn't afford to fill the tank, and she didn't know if she had enough gas to get me to school. After she dropped me off at school, her car sputtered to a stop and she had to call a friend to bring her gas to get to work. Looking back, it's kind of ironic, because at the same time my mom was worried about having enough gas to get me to school, people on YouTube were calling me a "spoiled bitch."

I started making money from YouTube when I became a YouTube partner. Being a YouTube partner basically means you can make money off of your videos through shared advertisement revenue, your channel has a lot more customizability like being able to put a cool banner on the top of it, and YouTube takes you a little bit more seriously. But back then you had to apply for it. I remember originally finding out about the program because I really wanted to know how some people had sick banners and channel designs, and I really wanted to make my channel look as cool as theirs. But while I don't remember the exact numbers you needed in order to qualify to be in the program, it was somewhere around a couple thousand subscribers and at least a hundred thousand views. I applied for partnership when I hit around 40,000 subscribers and got accepted. You'd only get a check when you made $100, so if you didn't make $100 in a month, it rolled over to the next month. In the beginning I would only get paid every three or four months, and it wouldn't be more than, like, $117. But every cent I made went back into YouTube. My parents did buy me my first camera, a Sony HDR-XR100, the last Christmas they were together. But I didn't get a new camera until I could afford to buy it for myself. I saved up all of my money for a couple years from YouTube, birthdays, and Christmases until I could afford to buy a Canon 60D. It was the first big purchase I ever made. It was the most rewarding feeling in the world to work so hard for something and finally get it. The crazy thing was, the next month I got my first big check from YouTube—for the exact amount I had paid for the camera.

You Tube Broadcast Yourself ™

help center | e-mail options | report spam

Dear jennxpenn,

Congratulations! Now that you're a YouTube partner, you're on your way to sharing revenue from your YouTube videos and increasing your audience through syndication.

Here's some important reference material. Please sign in to your YouTube account in order to access this information.

- **Getting Started Guide** - See how to use YouTube partner features.
- **Partner Tutorial** - Review the Partner Tutorial.
- **Partner Agreement** - Detailed partner agreement.
- **Community Guidelines** - Understand your responsibilities in ensuring a positive experience for our users.
- **Partner Account Settings** - Update your Google AdSense and Google Checkout information.

Looking for even more YouTube partner information? Visit our comprehensive Partner Help Center or catch the latest news in our blog.

Sincerely,
The YouTube Team

Still, even though I had started making more money, I hadn't really considered YouTube as a career, because I worried it wouldn't be secure enough. So when Mr. Hentz asked me what I wanted to do with my life, I said I wanted to go to school for psychology. He asked me why, and I told him that I was always reading articles about psychology online and it sounded pretty interesting, and psychologists make a good living. It wasn't a real answer. I didn't really want to be a psychologist, but it seemed like a good answer, at least good enough to get him to stop asking scary questions about my future. But then he asked, "So, are you going to study psychology because you like it or because you want a stable income?" Then I told him the truth. I just wanted to have a stable job. I thought he was going to be disappointed that I had just made something up, but he wasn't. Instead he just looked at me with this sympathetic smile and said,

"Do what you love and the money will follow."

Mr. Hentz's advice was so simple, but it totally changed the way I thought about my future. I knew what I loved; I loved making videos. I started thinking about going to college for film to improve my video quality, or even to business school to learn how to run my channel like a real company. For the first time, I was thinking about my future in terms of what I wanted my life to look like, not what I thought it should look like. I started taking my videos more seriously, and devoting more time to editing and coming up with ideas. By the end of sophomore year not only was I making more money from my videos, but I also signed my first big deal with my network, AwesomenessTV.

In June, I got an email from Shauna Phelan of Varsity Pictures, telling me that Brian Robbins was starting a new YouTube channel called AwesomenessTV and they wanted me to be a part of it. Now AwesomenessTV is not just a multi-channel YouTube network, but they also have a show on Nickelodeon, a management division, a clothing line at Kohl's, their own music label, and so much more. But back then, the channel didn't even exist yet. Still, I was super-excited about the email because Brian Robbins was one of the creators of *All That*, a sketch comedy show that used to be on Nickelodeon that was basically *Saturday Night Live* for kids. I was totally obsessed with that show. I knew it was a little risky to work with a company that hadn't even started yet, but they offered me a good deal and I took a chance. They wanted to pay me to make videos about anything I wanted and post them to their channel. Basically, they offered me money to do what I loved.

I always have that conversation with Mr. Hentz in the back of my mind when I'm making a big decision. When I decided to move to LA for my senior year, I thought about that conversation. When I was offered an obscene amount of money to make videos for a certain company, but my fans would have to pay for the content, I thought about that conversation and turned it down. Because even though it would've been an awesome paycheck, part of what I love is making videos that are equally accessible to anyone who wants to watch them. When I got my first starring role in a feature film, I thought about that conversation and how much it proved true to my life. I don't even think he knows it, but he changed my life.

So, Mr. Hentz, if you're reading this, thank you. I wouldn't be where I am today if it wasn't for you.

SOMETIMES . . .

1. BELIEVE You CAN & Your ½ way There.

2. DON'T TALK, JUST ACT.
DON'T SAY, JUST SHOW.
DON'T PROMISE, JUST PROVE

3. ASAP = ALWAYS SAY A PRAYER

4. It takes Nothing to Joint A CROWD, It takes everything to Stand Alone.

5. TRUE CONFIDENCE HAS NO Room FOR JEALOUSLY & ENVY. WHEN YOU KNOW YOUR GREAT, You HAVE NO Reason to HATE!

JENN —
Here A YOUR Pills
& Here is INSURANCE CARD,
PLEASE PLEASE GO place INTO YOUR CAR Right Now. Thanks MOM

Love You,
MOM ☺

FINDING
MY
VOICE

No one is born knowing exactly who he or she is. Seriously, nobody pops out of the womb thinking *I'm an extroverted vegetarian with a penchant for karaoke and an unhealthy obsession with plaid and guys with British accents.* Figuring out who you are is a process that begins long after they cut the umbilical cord.

You go through life trying on a bunch of identities, seeing what fits and what just kind of feels wrong.

I went through a lot of different phases before I found what fit. In elementary school I was obsessed with music. I played piano, violin, and even percussion. Once I realized I hated practicing and that was sort of a necessity for being a musician, I turned to writing. I would write little short stories, and I even started writing books (though this book you're reading is the first book I ever finished). Around the same time I was in band, I went through an artistic phase where I was obsessed with drawing, so I would bring a sketchbook to school every day. For a while I wanted to be an architect, like my grandpa, so I tried to draw blueprints and design houses. I even tried to be an animator. I had no idea what I was doing; I just downloaded a bunch of computer programs and I'd draw stuff on Microsoft Paint and try to animate it, but all of my attempts were so bad. They literally just looked like flipbooks with missing pages.

Even though I went through all those different phases, I've had two passions for as long as I can remember: taking pictures and making people laugh. Even before I was making videos, I would put on shows for my family members. I would create a stage in the front of the room out of dining room chairs. I'd announce that the show was starting, and I'd rip their tickets as they walked in. Then I would just tell jokes. Back then I didn't write my own material, but to be fair I was, like, eight. I had this SpongeBob joke book and I would stand on the stage made out of chairs and just read them straight from the book. I'm pretty sure the jokes weren't even that funny, but my parents sat through the whole thing and laughed at them regardless.

I've also had a passion for photography since I picked up my first camera around the age of four. Okay, so maybe it wasn't a real camera; it was a View-Master, you know, those toys that look like a mixture of a camera and binoculars, where you press a button on top that rotates through all these different mini-slides? My parents bought me one for Christmas and I became totally obsessed with it. But sometimes I wouldn't even look at the images on the slide-wheel; I would take them out and I would just look through the viewfinder and pretend I was taking photos. When I got older, my mom gave me her old DSLR camera and I would take pictures of everything. My favorite kinds of pictures to take were landscapes and close-ups (even though I couldn't afford a macro lens).

I think it is totally normal when you're a kid to want to try a bunch of different things. YouTube was sort of a natural choice for me because it allowed me to blend my interest in photography with my interest in making people laugh. But for me, figuring out what *kind* of YouTuber I wanted to be was kind of a similar process. After I started posting more to my channel, I experimented with the types of videos I made. And just like my interests when I was younger, I went through a lot of phases.

At first I mostly followed trends of what other YouTubers were doing, and a big trend back then was lip-dub videos. I thought it would be fun to try out, so I made a bunch when I was in eighth and ninth grade. My favorite ones were the two I made to Ellie Goulding songs: "Lights" and "Figure 8." Part of the reason is that she is my absolute favorite artist, but they were also my favorites because I spent a lot of time on the cinematography and was proud of the way they turned out. But posting lip-dub videos on YouTube came with a lot of drama, because some record labels view them as copyright infringement, so your video can get taken down and you can get strikes against your channel. YouTube is like baseball: Three strikes and you're out. I didn't want to risk getting my channel taken down, so I stopped. Until Meghan Camarena, a YouTuber who also made music videos at the time who I looked up to, contacted me on Twitter one day and asked if we

Lights - Ellie Goulding (Music Video)
by jennxpenn ☑
3 years ago • 596,120 views
Check out **Ellie Goulding** here: http://us.**elliegoulding**.com/ Buy this song here: http://tinyurl.com/6w5a759. Website ...
1:12 HD

Figure 8 - Ellie Goulding (Music Video)
by jennxpenn ☑
2 years ago • 231,451 views
Check out **Ellie Goulding** here: http://us.**elliegoulding**.com/ Buy this song here: http://tinyurl.com/curku3r. Website ...
1:17 HD

could talk over Skype. She basically told me she loved my music videos and that she had started working with a record label to get the rights to music by up-and-coming artists, and asked if I was interested in doing the same. From there on out I only made music videos to songs I had the rights to use, but I eventually stopped making them altogether to focus on another style of videos I liked making better.

I've never owned a beret, but I definitely went through an artsy phase. As I became a more skilled photographer, I started getting curious about what kinds of things I could do with different lenses, exposures, and aftereffects. For one of my videos I took a yellow highlighter and wrote my name in stop-motion. I edited it together, keyed out the yellow highlighter, and replaced the yellow with different colors and patterns so the letters looked like these shifting kaleidoscopes. My artsy videos were definitely out there, but I was proud of them because they were unique. However, they weren't always super-well-received, especially by kids at my school, so during points where my self-esteem dropped I deleted a lot of them.

After my artsy phase I sort of went through a "director" phase where I made a lot of short films. I wanted to feel like a real director, so I would stand in front of the camera, yell "action," do the scene, and then yell "cut," even if I was the only one in the shot. I was so lame. I made one about a snowman that comes to life and tries to kill me called "Snow Day." Another one was called "Serial Killer," where I go over to my friend's house, find her dead body, and don't realize the serial killer is still in the house. I'm just now realizing as I write this that I basically got murdered in almost all my short films. I liked making shorts but as I started to gain an audience, I wanted to vlog, because I wanted to talk directly to my viewers and because vlogs were what I liked to watch.

When I first started making videos, I didn't know vlogging was a thing. After being a part of MyCollab and FiveFreshTubers, I got more comfortable addressing the camera and started vlogging on my own channel. But my first vlogs didn't really have structures and were sort of pointless. I did this one called "Vlogging and Driving" where I pretended to be vlogging while pretending to be driving my mom's new car. But the rest of the video is me talking to the camera, like me telling people to get close to their computer so I can tell them a "secret," then screaming. In May of 2011, I made a separate vlog channel for random vlogging, because I wanted the posts on my main channel to be more organized. Also in May of 2011, I started a recurring show on my channel called *Ask Jenn*. People were always asking me questions on Facebook and Twitter, and sending me pictures of themselves on DailyBooth, this photo-based social media website in the pre-Instagram era, so I decided I would answer questions. I wanted to put a creative spin on it, so I created a bunch of different segments with transitions. As I started talking to the camera more, my channel grew more popular, and by December 21, 2011, I hit 100,000 subscribers.

Shortly after I hit the 100,000 milestone, I started to really find my vlogging style, which is really a mix of vlogging and sketch comedy (some people called it *sklogging*, but to me that word sort of sounds like someone's trying to say "clogging" while choking on their own saliva). I wasn't really aware I had found my style at the time, but looking back, the video I made in my second semester of sophomore year called "Friday the 13th" is when it started taking shape. In the video, I talked about how I didn't really believe in superstitions, and I made a list of things that were supposed to give you bad luck and I did them all on Friday the 13th, superstitiously the unluckiest day of the year. And for those of you wondering if breaking a mirror or walking under a ladder really brings you bad luck, they don't. For me, it was the exact opposite. Not only did I really like how that video turned out, but it did really well! Since the response was so great and I loved what I had created, I did the next video in a similar style and it also got a lot of views and positive comments.

From "Friday the 13th" on, my style started to become sort of what it is now. For those of you who aren't super-familiar with my channel, what I do now is vlog about a topic that's relatable to my life and I'll integrate a bunch of examples by cutting in short sketches. Part of the reason I think my style developed was because I was taking my channel way more seriously and I would spend a lot more time planning and executing my videos.

I get a lot of questions from aspiring YouTubers about what goes into making my videos. My process for making videos is actually pretty straightforward. I don't have any secret tips or a professional camera crew hiding in my bedroom closet. Unless I do a video for another channel, like AwesomenessTV, I do everything myself. Once I've come up with an idea for a video, I write down some bullet points. First I'll think, *Okay, the topic is types of friends, so I want to think of at least four sketch examples to go with that.* Then I'll quickly write down my ideas in a way that helps me organize my thoughts. I never write scripts, because it's just a lot of unnecessary work and I want the video to feel really natural.

After I have my notes, I'll get myself ready. When I no longer look like I just rolled out of bed, I set up my tripod and lights. I like my videos to look bright in the center and dark around the edges, so I use either a single softbox, which is a fabric box that diffuses light evenly, or a ring light, which is literally a ring of tiny lights that surrounds your lens. Then I do a test recording to make sure everything looks okay, and I'll check it, and fix the exposure.

After that, I'll film the entire segment where I am talking to the camera, pausing between sentences so it's easier for me to cut it up later. Even if I'm going to add skits in later, I go through the entire vlog part because, once I move the camera, it's really difficult to get it back in exactly the same spot. When I film skits by myself I usually do them after I vlog, but if I'm shooting with a friend, I sometimes film them before to suit my friend's schedule. It doesn't take that long because the skits are really quick, unless I'm shooting with Lauren Elizabeth, because we're constantly cracking up.

Next comes editing. First, I go through all of the vlog footage and do a rough cut, which means I cut the best takes together pretty sloppily. Then I'll go in and refine the cuts, which means I'll trim out the pauses and drag the audio so it blends together. I then pick the best takes from the sketch footage and edit it in where it belongs. At the end of it all, I'll add in music and graphics and color-correct the footage. When I'm done, I pick out a thumbnail and title for the video while I wait for it to render. This can take a few hours, but thankfully, as long as I check in and make sure there are no glitches, I don't actually have to sit there and watch it happen. Finally, the video is ready to upload to YouTube for all of you beautiful people to enjoy.

I know for those of you who just like watching videos for fun, and have no interest in becoming a YouTuber, those last couple of paragraphs may have read as somewhere between painfully boring and total gibberish. I'm sorry; you may want to take a snack break or something, because this next part is also for aspiring YouTubers.

There's one more type of video I still make today, and those are prank videos. I've always been a prankster for as long as I can remember. You know the story of the boy who cried wolf? I'm totally the girl who cried pregnant. I've told my mom I was pregnant so many times that by the time I actually am she probably won't believe me. I even filmed it once for a truth-or-dare video. I was filming at night like I often do, but she lives in the Eastern time zone while I'm in the Pacific time zone, so calling my mom at 10:00 p.m. actually meant I was calling her at 1:00 a.m. She was so tired and disoriented from me waking her up she actually believed me, and when I finally told her it was a joke she told me I almost gave her a heart attack.

And she swore she would get me back. To this day my mom is still my favorite target because she's so trusting that everything I say is true, or, in other words, she's gullible. Incidentally, my mom totally got me back for all the pranks I pulled on her. One morning she texted me and told me she had just landed in LA and asked if I could pick her up from the airport. The biggest range of emotions washed over me. At first I was excited to see her, then I suddenly got frustrated because she didn't tell me she was coming and I was totally unprepared for a houseguest. I was just about to attack the bathroom with some Clorox when she called me. She was laughing hysterically and kept repeating, "I got you back; I got you back so good." I should have known. It was literally April Fools' Day.

During my junior year, Meghan called me and told me Teen.com was relaunching their channel for a new season and wanted to give a bunch of different YouTubers the chance to make a 12-episode show. They helped me come up with a bunch of ideas for a show but ultimately I decided to make a prank show, called *Stranger Danger*. In March they flew me out to LA to film some of the episodes. They gave me a very tiny crew (Meghan and a sound guy), and my job was to come up with the ideas for the pranks and edit the videos together. The show premiered in May and did really well. It got a lot of views and *Huffington Post* even wrote an article about the first prank that was posted on the channel, called "One Direction Flirting." For the video, I went to Cal State Northridge and pretended to hit on guys using One Direction lyrics. A couple of guys saw the camera and knew I was recording but most of them really took me seriously.

People always ask if the way I am in my videos is the real me. It is—just an excited version of me. When I get excited about something in real life, my voice gets elevated and louder, I talk with my hands a lot, and my face gets super-expressive. And while there have definitely been some videos where I don't seem super-excited (usually because I am super-tired), most of the time I'm that excited version of myself because I genuinely love making videos. When I turn the camera on, that passion just sort of takes over. No matter what someone's interest is, if they're passionate about it when they speak, I'm always interested in listening. Like, I don't really enjoy watching sports on TV like hockey, but my mom loves it. When she

TOP 10 TIPS FOR BECOMING A SUCCESSFUL YOUTUBER

1. CHOOSE A CREATIVE NAME

When you're choosing your YouTube username, you want to pick something you REALLY like. That name is going to stick with you for the rest of your YouTube career. I have a lot of friends that started posting on YouTube when they were very young, and they chose names they sort of regret. You can kind of change the name of your channel, but unless you want to build your subscribers up from scratch, you're sort of stuck with your username.

2. DECIDE WHAT VIDEOS YOU WANT TO MAKE

Make the kind of videos you like to watch, but also do something you're good at or you think is fun. I don't make beauty videos because I am definitely not good at makeup. I kind of just put stuff on my face where I think it should go. I hate curling my hair; I'll do, like, half my head and I'll get bored. If I have an event or I just want to dress up, I turn to the beauty gurus in my life for help. That's one of the many advantages of having Arden Rose and Lauren Elizabeth as roommates. There's always someone there to curl the other half of my head.

3. GET INVOLVED IN THE COMMUNITY

If you leave a lot of comments (positive comments) on other people's videos, other users will start to recognize your name and want to check out your channel. Also, make friends with other YouTubers. It's not too hard; I mean, you already know you have something in common. Form a collab channel or film a collab with another YouTuber. I already gave you the Top 10 Tips for Asking Someone to Collab. (Come on, guys, I'm giving you so much to work with here!)

4. KEEP A NOTEBOOK OF IDEAS

I wish every week I just woke up and thought, *Damn, I have the perfect idea for this week's video*. But that doesn't always happen. Sometimes I get, like, a flood of ideas in one day, and sometimes, well . . . not so much. So since eighth grade, I started keeping a notebook of ideas, so when I hit a week where the ideas just aren't coming, I can flip back through my notebook and use one I came up with weeks before. I carry my notebook around with me basically all the time in case I get ideas in random places. (You never know what is going to inspire you.) I'm kind of old-fashioned when it comes to taking notes. I don't know why, I just like writing stuff out by hand. But if that doesn't work for you, keep a list of video ideas in your phone. I use my phone as my backup notebook when I go places where other people might think carrying a notebook is weird, like a birthday party or a concert. Though, for the record, I don't really think carrying a notebook anywhere is weird.

5. PHOTOGRAPHY 101

A lot of successful YouTubers don't know how to properly use a camera. Today, you don't really need to. Almost everything can be fixed in post. But I pride myself on knowing how to properly set up the lighting and exposure, and I think it really makes a difference. Even if you can create the perfect shot on your computer, it's easier if you just get it right the first time, especially when it comes to lighting. Even if you can't afford fancy lights, everyone has access to one awesome light: It's called the sun. You can make a well-lit video if you set up your camera in front of a window so the sunlight shines on your beautiful face. Before I could afford lights, I shot a lot of my videos outside to take advantage of the free lighting.

6. CREATE A SCHEDULE

Consistency is one of the most important things to creating a successful channel. I post on Saturdays, which means every Saturday my subscribers can expect a new video from me and they know to go check it out. If you don't post for a few weeks, people may stop coming back to your channel. Trust me, I know it can be challenging to come up with a new idea every week, even if you are keeping a notebook, but it's definitely possible. If you're having a lot of trouble with this, ask someone for some ideas.

7. CLEAN YOUR ROOM

If you're going to shoot videos in your room, you should probably pick your underwear off the floor. Obviously, a clean background looks more professional, but more than that, it makes people focus on you. If the background of your video is super-cluttered, people aren't going to be watching you; they are going to be looking at the weird stain on that sweatshirt on your floor. When people watch your videos you want them to think, *Wow, that kid's awesome*, not *I wonder if that's ketchup or blood*.

8. SPEND TIME EDITING

I'm not saying you have to spend an entire day locked in a dark room like some reclusive crazy person or, you know, me. But take your time. I think adding in a couple mistakes or outtakes can be fun, but if you leave in the part where you adjusted your lights for, like, three minutes, your audience is going to get bored. And don't worry if no one's giving you a "World's Greatest Editor" mug for your birthday yet. Everyone starts somewhere. My videos were so poorly edited in the beginning. Actually, they weren't even edited in the beginning. It's a skill that just takes practice.

9. GOOD TITLES AND THUMBNAILS

Titles and thumbnails are super-important because they're the two things people actually see before they decide to watch your video. Pick an interesting image for the thumbnail and make the titles pop by using cool graphics. Make sure both the title and the thumbnail actually relate to your video. I know "Nicki Minaj Bitch-slaps Kim Kardashian" seems like a great title to get people to click on your video, and you'll probably get a lot of people to watch, but if your video is really a vlog about your day at the beach, not one of those people will come back next week to watch "Selena Gomez Streaks Through Disneyland."

10. DO IT FOR FUN

People who make YouTube videos just to make money generally don't make money. Viewers can tell they're not in it for the right reasons, and they don't like it. Every big YouTuber does some branded videos, because in the end, YouTube is our job, but if every single video you're doing is a branded video, it's like your channel is just one big advertisement. And who wants to watch that? I only do branded videos if I genuinely like the product. I've been offered brand deals that I didn't take because they didn't feel like me. I once got a weird email from a sex-toy company asking me to do a branded video. I'm pretty sure I don't have to explain why I turned that one down. But I've also turned down branded videos for products I love because there were too many strings attached. Some companies are way too overbearing and want to tell you exactly what to say. Those are deal breakers.

talks about it I don't mind listening, because she's so genuinely excited about it, but then I watch a game and I remember how boring it is to me. Whenever I think someone's interest is weird, I always think, *Well, I make videos on the Internet.*

My voice has definitely changed a bit over the years. When I was younger I was not just Excited Me, I was High-Pitched, Extra-Hyper Excited Me. Strangely enough, some of my viewers miss that jumping, screaming, hyperactive thirteen-year-old. She's still here; she just grew up. I'm nineteen now; if I were running around and screaming like I did when I was thirteen, you would probably think I was psychotic.

> Growing up is just a part of life, and with growing up comes change.

I like to think that my videos cover topics that my audience can relate to. And while my voice may change as I get older, I hope that part never does. The coolest thing to me is that my subscribers are growing up with me. (Unless one of you took a bath in the fountain of youth or became a vampire or something, but there's really nothing I can do about that.)

A TALE OF
TWO VIDCONS

Two VidCons, both alike in dignity, in fair Anaheim where we lay our scene . . . Wait, hold up, no. That's not *A Tale of Two Cities*, that's *Romeo and Juliet*. But even if it was the right opening line, VidCon 2012 and VidCon 2013 were definitely not "alike in dignity." In the time between these two conventions, my life changed dramatically. Not only did my channel more than double in subscribers, but I had also started flying to LA to film collabs; I had my own shows on AwesomenessTV and Teen.com; I was attending video conventions as an invited guest; and, most importantly, I found real friends both on YouTube and at school. By VidCon 2013, my life was, well, to put it simply, just so much better. But VidCon 2012, well, to quote the actual opening line from *A Tale of Two Cities*, "It was the best of times, it was the worst of times." (Okay, I'll stop referencing books you've been forced to read in English class now.)

For those of you who don't know that much about VidCon, John Green, author of *The Fault in Our Stars* and other amazing books, and his brother, Hank, also known as the Vlogbrothers, came up with the idea in 2010 as a way for members of the online video community to get together and celebrate our weird and amazing culture. VidCon is a place where fans can interact with one another as well as their favorite YouTube and Vine celebrities, attend panel discussions, concerts, and parties, and pretty much just hang out. For a lot of YouTubers, the first time they attend VidCon is when they get invited as a professional, but in 2012, I went to my first VidCon as a fan.

I can't even describe how excited I was to go to VidCon 2012.

California was the place I had wanted to visit more than anywhere else in the world, and I was finally going. I hadn't been on planes a lot, so even going to the airport felt exciting. (I had flown so little in my life that when I saw a plastic bag on my seat on the plane, I said, "What's that?" and when my mom told me it

who else is going to vidcon? i'll be in LA from june 28th-july 3rd! who's going to meet me this summer!? :)

↩ ⇄ ★ ⋯

was a blanket I was like, "Wow, that's so cool." About an airplane blanket. Seriously.) But I was mostly excited because it was my first Internet event. After three years posting videos, I felt very much a part of the YouTube community, even if only a small part. And VidCon 2012 was the first time I was going to get to hang out with my community in real life.

But it was in some ways "the worst of times" because I brought Veronica, and she tried her hardest to ruin it for me—at least that's what it seemed like. At that point I knew she had been talking shit about me, but we had purchased plane tickets and VidCon tickets months before and it was too late to back out. I hadn't confronted her yet, but the tension definitely hung over us when we were in California. Veronica was the kind of person who always wanted to be the center of attention. But at VidCon there was definitely more attention focused on me, and she hated it. That was my world and she wasn't a part of it. Veronica started acting super-bitchy halfway through the trip. My mom had been very clear that she wanted us to stick together, especially since it was her responsibility to watch Veronica, but Veronica disregarded my mom's rules and kept wandering off. She made the day about her because I constantly had to search for her. I had stopped to talk to some people and Veronica just walked away, and I had no idea where she went. Later, after I located her and we went to Mitchell Davis's panel, I don't remember exactly what happened, but Veronica got super-pissed because I sat in the chair she had wanted to sit in, and she stormed off. She wouldn't answer her phone. She wouldn't respond to texts. And for a hot second I was actually kind of worried something happened to her. Nothing did. She was just being super-dramatic. VidCon was the last thing Veronica and I ever did together before our friendship ended.

Aside from, like, the total dissolution of my relationship with one of my best friends, the trip was also "the best of times." VidCon draws in YouTubers and fans from all over the world, so I knew I was going to get to see a lot of my YouTube friends. I had been iChatting with a bunch of YouTubers for a long time, but VidCon 2012 was the first time I met them in person. I met all of the guys from O2L before they were O2L, and some of my international YouTuber friends, like Patrick Quirk from Canada, and Jack Matthews from England. Meeting people I only knew from the Internet was kind of surreal. You don't really think about it when you're watching people's videos, but for most of them you've never seen the lower half of their bodies, so there's this weird moment when you first see them in person where you're like, "Whoa, you have legs."

I also met a beauty guru named Alexa Losey for the first time, who pretty much changed my life because she's given me tons of great advice and she's the person who introduced me to half of my best friends today. Veronica, Patrick, Jack, and I snuck into a greenroom for "special guests," and we randomly started a conversation with her. She and I kept in touch and talked a lot on Facebook after that. That first night of the convention we attended a party hosted by District Lines. I wasn't on the list, but we snuck in through the back entrance and got into the party, where I got to meet Ian Hecox and Anthony Padilla from Smosh. They were literally the reason I started posting on YouTube, and it was such a surreal experience to meet them and tell them how much they'd inspired me. I thought the weekend couldn't get any better. But it did.

The next day, VidCon officially started, and we got to see and do so many amazing things. Just walking through the expo hall, we met a ton of YouTubers and we even ran into Ian and Anthony, who recognized me from the night before (lifelong dream fulfilled), and later we saw them perform on the main stage. I also met Rebecca Black in person for the first time. We weren't as close then as we are now, but we had video chatted a bit. Her video for "Friday" had come out a year before, and while a lot of people hated on that video, a ton of people wanted to meet her, because she had a *huge* line for her meet-and-greet in the expo hall. Because we were (kind of) friends with her, we ran past the line to say hi, which I realize was kind of an asshole-y move. But she saw us coming toward her and called us over.

That day I also did some of my first interviews. Meghan Camarena, a YouTube gamer, vlogger, singer-songwriter, and comedian, was conducting interviews for Teen.com. We became friends from talking about lip-dubbing on Skype, so she interviewed me, asking me the most random questions, like "What's the grossest food that you've ever eaten?" Then I was walking by this booth called YouNow, and they asked me how many subscribers I had, and when I told them, they had Michael Buckley interview me, which was super-exciting because he was one of the original YouTube celebrities known for pop culture commentary. He's continued to be supportive of my channel since then and I consider him a good friend; he's one of the nicest and most helpful people I've met in the community.

My trip to California for VidCon totally met if not exceeded my expectations. I attended cool panels, met a bunch of YouTube celebrities, and Veronica, Jack, Patrick, and I even snuck onstage during a dance party. Also, I got a chance to visit the AwesomenessTV offices for the first time. But the one thing I didn't expect was that I would get recognized. Aside from getting recognized by people at school, which basically made my life hell, I had only ever been recognized a few times before. But at VidCon I was so excited to see YouTubers I watched, it seriously never occurred to me that there would be people excited to see me.

At that point I had over 100,000 subscribers, but until you've actually met fans in person, it just sort of feels like a number. Like, obviously, I know my subscribers are real people; I respond to comments and tweets, and I see all the different usernames. But it's totally different when someone comes up to you and asks for you to take a picture with them. The first time it happened, we were just walking into our hotel and this girl was like, "Are you Jenn?" and pulled out her camera. We took a picture with her and I acted like it was no big deal, but inside I was freaking out. It was the best feeling ever. I was definitely way more excited to meet my fans than they were to meet me, and I mean that in the best possible way. Throughout VidCon, fans came up to me and asked me to take pictures and sign autographs. It was so cool to put faces to the usernames. I was even a little nervous signing autographs; I didn't even know how to sign my name. Now my signature looks the same every time, but back then I was all over the place. I started writing my name out perfectly in cursive, but that took too long. I experimented with signing my name a bunch of different ways. So if your friend says she has an autograph from me from 2012 and it looks nothing like my signature, she's not lying to you (probably).

But by far the coolest thing that happened was when I met Shane Dawson, one of my favorite YouTube comedians. Shane has always been one of my favorite YouTubers, so I made Jack, Patrick, and Veronica wait in line for, like, an hour to meet him. But when I saw him and he, in his words, "screamed like a little girl," it was super-validating. In reality, he just smiled and said, "Hey, I watch you" (obviously, I have it on video), but that was enough. At that time Shane had over 2,700,000 subscribers. That's a lot, even by today's standards, but to put that in perspective, the most-subscribed channel at the time only had 5,400,000. Basically, Shane was (and still is) a super-big deal . . . and he knew who I was. Then he said into my camera for my video that week, "If you're not subscribed to her, you should; I am." I couldn't believe it. He had actually seen my videos. Watching the footage of me meeting him now that I know Shane a little better, it's really funny. Even though we both have big, loud personalities on YouTube, we're both sort of shy and introverted around new people. In the video we're both nervously shifting our weight from foot to foot, shyly complimenting each other. He told me I was super-creative. I told him he was super-funny. We had an awkward side-hug. But that moment sealed a feeling that had been building up all weekend.

This was where I belonged.

But if even part of VidCon 2012 was the best of times, VidCon 2013 was like the best-est of times. (Yes, I realize that's not a word.) Basically, each Internet event I attended over the course of the year that followed reconfirmed the feeling that I belonged way more in the YouTube universe than I ever did in high school. I was still a fan of other YouTubers—I will always be a fan of other YouTubers—but as my channel grew, I started to feel more like the professionals I had met and looked up to at the first VidCon. And by the time I got to VidCon 2013, I just was one of them.

By VidCon 2013 I really understood what it means to attend these events as a professional. That year, Andrea Russett and I drove down to Anaheim together. About a month before VidCon 2013, I had moved

to LA for the summer. Technically, Playlist Live 2013 (an event created by the company District Lines as an East Coast answer to VidCon) was the first event I attended as a professional, but immediately when we got there I realized that this VidCon was going to be different. Industry Day hadn't even started yet and I had already taken more pictures with fans and signed more autographs than I did during all of Playlist (okay, maybe that's a bit of an exaggeration, but it was close).

I had always wondered why you barely ever saw the bigger YouTubers wandering around the expo hall, going to different booths and getting swag like everyone else. That VidCon I learned why: You can't. Andrea and I and a couple of our friends tried to explore the convention to check out our friend's booth, and we got completely mobbed. It was such a cool feeling and at first we just stood in the middle of the mob taking pictures, filming short videos, and giving hugs, but then a security guard came and rushed us out. We didn't understand why at first; it's not like our fans were violent psychopaths waiting to hack us up with machetes. You guys are the best. And then he explained why: Apparently, we were causing a fire hazard. The fire marshal has strict rules about large crowds blocking exits and we had violated, like, all of them. We couldn't even go to the little food court inside the hotel without causing a scene. The only time I really got to see the expo hall was as part of a group "Hangout" for Teen.com. By that time I had started a pranking show for Teen.com, and they had me and the stars of their other shows hang out on a beach blanket set up on this platform, under a fake palm tree. We answered fan questions about our shows. It was supes-casual; we had, like, a bowl of Red Vines in the middle. I was a little jealous of the fans that got to walk around getting free stuff and meeting their favorite YouTubers, but it was still cool to feel a sense of shift in my life. And, when you attend these events as a content creator, there are private parties, so I still got to see YouTubers I admired, but this time I was getting to meet them as peers and most of them were already my friends.

At VidCon 2013 I was on a panel with other YouTubers from AwesomenessTV; although I had been on a panel at Playlist Live, this was the first time I felt like I was on a panel with my peers. When I was on my first panel at Playlist, I was super-nervous because it reminded me of, like, a group discussion in high school, and you guys now know how much I *loved* talking in front of the class. I was also the youngest person on the panel by far. Even though they were all really nice to me and let me talk as much as they did, I had this weird feeling like they were the experts and I was the panel's awkward little sister. But at VidCon I was on a panel with people my age who felt more on my level.

I also did a meet-and-greet with the rest of my friends at AwesomenessTV, and it was the first time I really felt like everyone in line knew exactly who I was. At one point during Playlist, I had tweeted my location in the expo hall and, like, thirty fans came and found me, but that was the closest I had to a meet-and-greet. It was hard to get used to meeting fans because I didn't know what to say; I was just so overwhelmed by the support and love, and I felt like I was a little awkward. I still get nervous before meet-and-greets. I don't want them to get their hopes up and then be like, "Wow, she's kinda lame."

My first real meet-and-greet was at DigiFest NYC, which is a daylong festival put on by DigiTour Media. But at DigiFest they put all the YouTubers behind one long table and fans go down the line and theoretically say hi to everybody. It's a cool concept because fans get to meet everyone at once without having

TOP 10 BEST MOMENTS FROM VIDCONS 2012 AND 2013

1. Being interviewed for the first time

2. Being recognized by a couple of people who watched my videos

3. Being invited as a guest to VidCon

4. Speaking on a panel with a bunch of my friends

Name: JENN McALLISTER

Channel/Company: JENNxPENN

Passion:

5. Flying to California for the first time (and also just generally flying somewhere farther west than Illinois for the first time)

38196 feet
Temperature: -76 degrees Fahrenheit

6. Meeting all of my Internet friends in person for the first time

7. Meeting Smosh, the two guys whose channel inspired the start of mine

8. The Teen.com "Hangout"

9. Doing my first official meet-and-greet with a bunch of my friends

10. Penny boarding through the parking garages at the VidCon hotel with some friends during our downtime

to stand in, like, seven different lines. But because it's *everyone's* fans, some people just sort of nonchalantly skip you and it feels super-awkward. But at VidCon 2013, partly because I was on a panel with other kids from AwesomenessTV, and partly because my fan base had grown by another 50,000 subscribers since DigiFest NYC, I felt like I wasn't getting skipped. We were signing autographs for over two hours. We didn't have time for lunch, so I literally had to eat a sandwich and sign autographs at the same time. But more than not getting skipped, or signing so many autographs I thought my hand was going to fall off, it just felt different. A year before, I had been the one standing in line, telling YouTubers they were my inspiration and asking Shane Dawson to give a shout-out on my vlog. Suddenly, fans coming down the line told me that *I* inspired *them* and asked me to give shout-outs on their vlogs. And that felt awesome.

HIGH SCHOOL'S SMALL, THE WORLD IS BIG

There are more than seven *billion* people in the world; I'm not exaggerating, more than seven *billion*. Even if you go to the biggest high school in America, there are only eight thousand people. Most high schools only have around one thousand. If you factor in how many people are in your grade, and then how many people are in the classes you take, you're really only looking at a population of, like, two hundred people that you have to deal with on a daily basis—two hundred out of seven billion people in the world. Not to get all statistical on you, but the probability that you are going to find "your people" in high school is basically zero. You have a slightly better chance of winning the lottery. Okay, so maybe that *is* an exaggeration, because some of those seven billion people are babies, some are super-old, some speak other languages, and some are in jail or something, but my point is this: If you are sitting in the middle of your cafeteria and you feel like no one understands you and that you'll never find a place where you fit in, remember high school is small and the world is big.

You have a place in it, even if you haven't found it yet.

Mid–sophomore year, something shifted and people stopped yelling at me in the halls. Suddenly, people started thinking it was "cool" rather than "stupid" that I had a YouTube channel. Occasionally, people would still make jokes like "Oh my god, you're so famous," but it wasn't with the same tone they had used before. I'd like to think people just grew up, but that wasn't it; it was my subscriber count that did the growing. It turns out 110,000 subscribers was the magic number! People stopped wanting to tear me down; instead, they started wanting things from me. It was nice not to be yelled at in the halls anymore, but I just wanted to fit in, to be treated like everyone else. And it became super-clear that was never going to happen.

The same people who had been yelling, "Your videos suck," literally a year before were asking me to edit their videos now. When we were assigned a video project in Spanish, everyone wanted to be my partner regardless of whether or not we had ever spoken to each other. I'm always down for making videos with my friends; I shoot collabs or help friends out with their videos all the time. Junior year, when "Harlem Shake" videos were a thing, I shot and edited my high school's edition, even posted it to my channel. Our video got *waaay* more views than our rival high school's version did, and even though most days I couldn't wait for last bell, I was still happy to create something everyone in my school was proud of. But it's really hard to want to make videos or create graphics for people who spent the previous two years trying to tear you down.

There's a chance I was being a little overly paranoid and that some of the people who were being super-nice and asking me to hang out with them actually just wanted to hang out with me. I definitely had some trust issues. But by this point I had discovered that the people I called friends, well, weren't really friends at all.

I think a lot of people in high school, especially girls, stay friends with people who chip away at their self-esteem because it just feels easier than having to try and make new ones. At a certain point I felt more like myself in my videos than I did walking down the halls of my high school, because in high school there is tremendous pressure to be like everyone else. But during my junior year, being like everyone else stopped

seeming so important, as I realized—partially through new school friends and partially through my YouTube friends—that high school is a very small place. The world's a lot a bigger than high school.

Junior year I found two friends who helped me feel like I could be myself at school: Jordyn and Gabriela. I met them freshman year because we were all in a lot of Honors classes, but we didn't really hang out outside of school until the end of sophomore year. Every year Jordyn held a bonfire where she literally set all of her class notes on fire, and at the end of the school year she invited me to come burn all of my notes. When I started writing this chapter I had no idea how to describe Jordyn and Gabriela. I even called them to ask what they'd want me to say about them and they just said, "Tell them we're the coolest fucking people you've ever met." And while true, that wasn't super-helpful.

But I think people's actions demonstrate their character better than anything else.

Even when putting me down was trendier than Juicy tracksuits and Uggs (ew), they never participated. Not once. If they heard people laughing about me they would let those people know that they weren't actually all that funny. Whenever I had to stay in on a Friday night to finish a video, they totally understood. But even when they knew I had to work, they still invited me, so I knew I was always included. If I was stuck on video ideas, they would help me brainstorm. Even now they'll be in my videos if I ask them, even though I made Jordyn throw up in my "Bean Boozled Challenge" video this year, where you had to pick random jelly beans by color and you didn't know if they would taste like peaches or actual vomit. Okay, I kind of forced her into filming that one, but she still did it. I may have taught them a few things about how to make YouTube videos over the years (or that you should never say yes to a best friend challenge unless you are prepared to have an egg cracked over your head), but they taught me something *way* more important. They taught me what it was like to have *real* friends.

The other people who made me really comfortable being myself were my YouTube friends. People often comment about how it seems like all the big YouTubers know one another, and that's because we do. When we started, YouTube was so much smaller and nobody really understood it except us. Even though we'd never actually met in person, my YouTube friends and I bonded quickly because we shared common interests and experiences. We all understood what it was like to be a YouTuber in high school. While meeting your friends online may sound weird, in some ways it wasn't all that different from how you'd make friends in real life. Some days I'd be talking to Tyler Cleary and he would just add someone else into our iChat, just like if you were meeting your friend at the mall or something, and they brought along another friend.

Through working with Teen.com I became good friends with Meghan Camarena and Joey Graceffa. When I'd come to LA to film videos without my mom, I'd stay with Meghan. She's like a big sister to me, and I couldn't imagine what my life would be like if I had never met her. Joey and I had known each other from when he was a Sunday guest on MyCollab, but we started hanging out more when I'd stay with Meghan because they've always been super-close. I was a little intimidated by Joey at first because he's also a comedy vlogger, he's a little older than me, and has about double the amount of subscribers as me—he's basically me but just a couple years ahead—but he's also so incredibly nice. I still look up to Joey professionally, but personally he's someone I know I can always talk to if I need some advice.

Between VidCon 2012 and Playlist 2013 I had made so many friends, and by the time we saw each other at Playlist, it was like I had the tight-knit group of friends I'd been searching for. I met Jack Baran, one of my best friends, in person for the first time. Jack and I had talked a lot online and he was super-nervous he wasn't going to have anyone to hang out with at the event, so he DMed me asking if he could hang out with me. Of course I said yes, and the rest is history. After hanging out a lot at Playlist, we started a giant group chat that included a bunch of YouTubers including the guys from O2L, Andrew Lowe, and Andrea Russett, and as we made more friends we added them into the group. We texted every single day and I got to know all of them really well. Like, I learned Ricky Dillon is quite possibly the world's nicest human. And that Andrew has the driest sense of humor, to the point where he makes my dry sense of humor look like a waterfall or something else not dry. The chat kept us all in touch even though we were all in different states, and it's what really brought us closer together as friends.

Most of us had plans to move to LA that summer, and once I got there we all became inseparable. The first day I showed up, I had to film a prank video for my show *Stranger Danger*, and Jc Caylen and Connor Franta offered to help. Jc was great for pranking because he's always really fun and is always down for everything. He helped me hit on strangers using Bruno Mars lyrics, and Connor happily held the camera and filmed it for me. Kian moved up to LA a little later. Kian's always been a little crazy and super-funny, but he's also really caring. He's the kind of guy that always makes sure I'm okay. Although I've always known about his videos, I met Anthony Quintal when Jack brought him to one of O2L's parties. We bonded over this totally ridiculous Vine account and exchanged numbers literally just so we could keep making jokes about the Vines.

In a funny way I can sort of divide my friends into two categories: those I met through Alexa Losey, and those I didn't. The first list is most definitely longer. Rebecca Black became one of my best friends when I moved to LA. She had always been close with Alexa, so even though she was still in high school (she'll graduate by the time this book comes out . . . CONGRATS, BEX!), she would come up from Orange County every weekend

to hang out. When Andrea and I moved in together, Rebecca would come sleep over basically every weekend. The tradition continued when we moved into a house with Arden Rose and Lauren Elizabeth. We call her our unofficial fifth roommate.

Through Alexa I also met Lauren and Arden, but I became better friends with those two when I moved into the same apartment complex in LA as them. Lauren and I quickly became best friends because we're so similar to each other. We both have really dry senses of humor, so we can be really sarcastic together. Lauren is someone that I could never imagine not being friends with. We do practically everything together, have gone through so many highs and lows together, and we can trust each other with anything.

YouTube is a unique community in that we really don't have to compete with one another. Our channels are not like TV networks competing for DVR space. With users in every time zone, there is no hour of the day when someone is not watching a YouTube video. The subscriber base is basically infinite and includes anyone with an Internet connection or a cell phone. And people can subscribe to as many channels

TOP 10 SIGNS YOU'VE FOUND THE RIGHT FRIENDS

1. TRUST ME

More than anything, you need to be able to trust your friends. I trusted Claire and Grace with my secret about my YouTube channel, and they created a hate account for me so . . . so much for that. I trusted that Veronica wasn't a total bitch, and . . . well . . . But I've trusted Gabriela and Jordyn with so many personal things, and they have never once let me down.

2. NO PEER PRESSURE

Again, you know, don't do drugs. But also don't be friends with people who would ask you to do something that just isn't you. Fitting in is like a defense mechanism, and with friends, you shouldn't need to defend yourself. That's one of the things I love the most about Anthony. He is so one hundred percent himself, he makes it super-easy to be one hundred percent myself. I love him to death.

3. MAKE YOU A BETTER PERSON

Right now, both Gabriela and Jordyn are starting their second semesters at Ivy League schools. One of the things that's awesome about Gabriela and Jordyn is that they've always been super-motivated. The same is true with my YouTube friends, like Connor Franta for example. He is such a creative and hardworking guy who I know has big things ahead of him in the future. Motivation is highly contagious. If you surround yourself with motivated people, you will find yourself working harder almost by accident.

4. GO TEAM

Your friends should be cheerleaders. And I don't mean the kind of cheerleaders that wear short skirts and stand on the sidelines at basketball games and say things like "Be aggressive! Bee Eee aggressive!" I mean they should be your personal cheerleaders who genuinely want you to succeed in everything you do. Meghan's always offering me cool opportunities, taking me under her wing, and giving me some of the best advice I've ever received.

5. NONVERBAL COMMUNICATIONS

Communication is important and you can't expect that your friends know exactly how you feel every single second without telling them. But with really good friends you can sort of tell how they're feeling just from their eyes. Lauren and I are really good at having nonverbal conversations. Sometimes I'll be in a situation where I'm super-uncomfortable and I can just look at Lauren, and she gets that I mean "Dude, this is super-awkward."

6. COME AS YOU ARE

Friends shouldn't care what you look like. Real friends love you, even in those ugly sweatpants and that T-shirt that has a hole in the armpit. The same is true with emotions. Real friends let you come as you are. If I'm anxious, tired, frustrated, angry, whatever, Rebecca is my go-to when I need to vent. Without her in my life, I'd probably go insane. Andrew's also become a super-calming force in my life. I often room with him at YouTube events, because in a high-stress situation I know I can count on Andrew to make me chill out.

7. YOU ALWAYS HAVE FUN

Obviously, life is not Disneyland. And even at Disneyland, sometimes there are really long lines that make you super-miserable. But with real friends you can always find a way to make things fun. Good friends can make you laugh even when you feel like crying. They help you see the comedy in even the darkest situations. Trevor is absolutely crazy and can always make me cry from laughter. I consider him a little brother because he's the youngest of my friends, and I would honestly do anything for him.

8. BRUTAL HONESTY

I know I made a super-big deal about Veronica making fun of my prom dress, but I want to be clear why: I don't care if she hated my prom dress; I care that she said, "Oh my god, you look so pretty" to my face and then said, "Oh my god, she looks like shit" behind my back. You don't want friends who tell you what they think you want to hear. You want friends who will tell you like it is. I love when my friends tell me I look like shit, because when they do it's because it's true, and that's why I love them so much.

9. YOU CAN TALK ABOUT ANYTHING

And I mean anything. Like even weird medical stuff. Jack and I are so close and have known each other for so long there is nothing I can't tell him. We're similar, so we really understand each other's feelings and emotions. We've also had a similar journey moving from the East Coast to LA, so he's easy to relate to. He's always been there for me when I've needed him the most.

10. KNOW YOU—LIKE, REALLY KNOW YOU.

Your true friends know things about you that not just anyone knows. Whether it's your deepest, darkest secret or your weird, creepy obsession, they know the real you and they appreciate and love you for exactly who you are. Lauren knows me so well it's like sometimes she knows what I'm going to do before I even do it. It's kinda scary.

as they want, so it's not like if someone subscribes to one YouTuber, they can't also subscribe to me. When YouTubers collab, they share their audience with one another, which is a win-win situation.

We're a community that works best when we grow together.

Not all YouTubers are the same, but it seems like we all share a certain quality that bonds us together. I don't really know what to call it, but there's some kind of unnamed thing that everyone has that made us post our first videos and keep going. I think a lot of us are kind of similar, and maybe even a little introverted, because we spent a lot of time sitting in our rooms, alone, talking to our cameras. But maybe it's just this: YouTube gave us our place in the world.

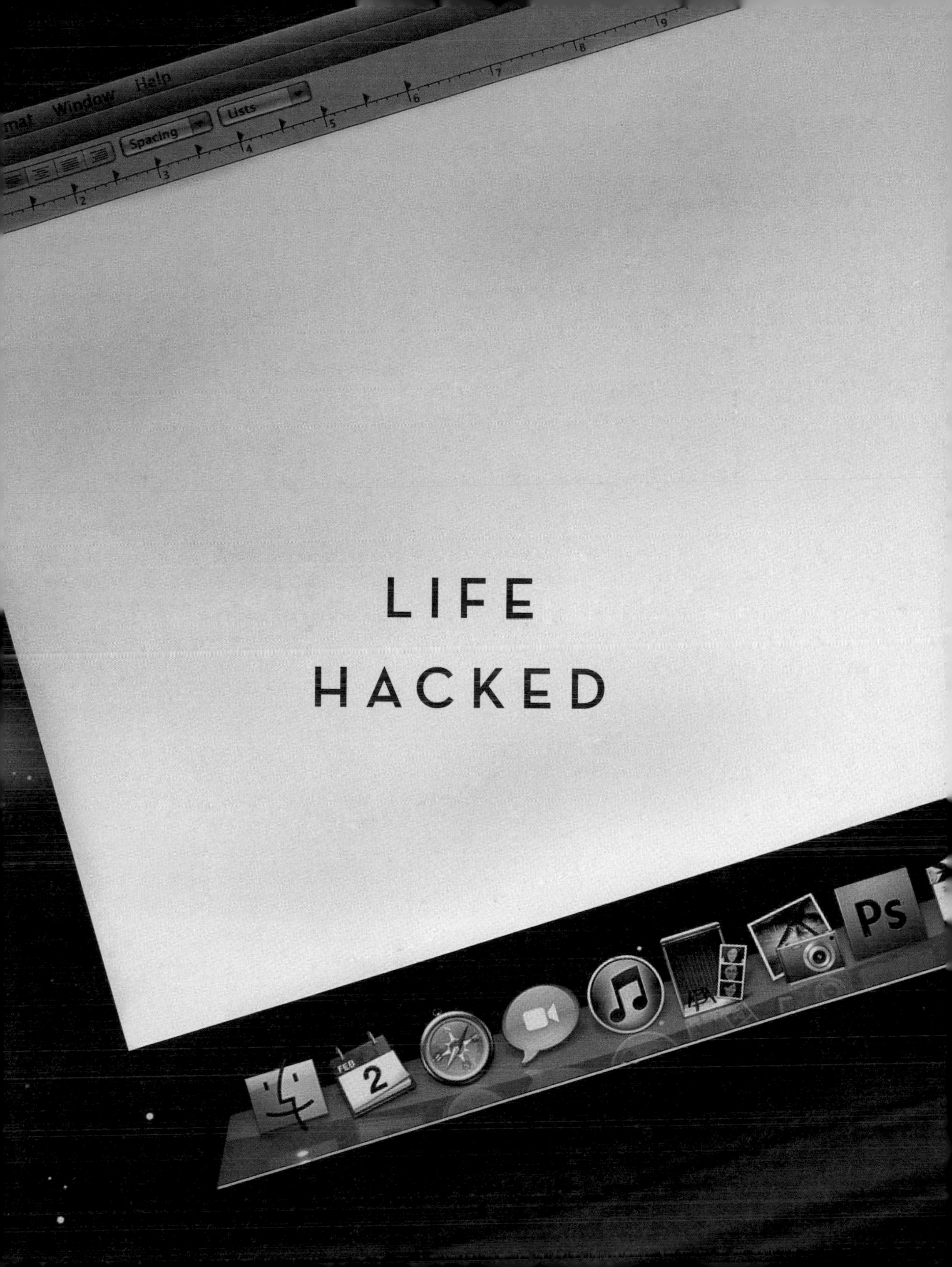
Window
Help
Spacing
Lists
LIFE
HACKED
FEB
2
Ps

On September 8, 2012, my YouTube channel got hacked. It's something I've never really talked about publicly before because it was a really upsetting and terrifying period of my life. Of course, part of me wanted to share this with the Internet, but the other part of me was too afraid to even talk about it. I'm going to share it with you guys now because ultimately it's part of my story and it's important to know these things can happen.

Around 4:00 a.m., Ricky Dillon called and texted me like a million times. Ricky was in college at the time; it was a Friday night (technically, Saturday morning) and he was always awake weird hours in the night, so a 4:00 a.m. call didn't immediately trigger the thought that something might be wrong. I was obviously sleeping, so I didn't answer. He then repeatedly called my landline until my mom answered. She was also asleep, so she groggily wandered into my room and said, "Ricky is on the phone. He says he really needs to talk to you." My eyes burned from the light, but I grabbed the phone.

"They're deleting everything," he said, and explained that a few minutes before he called, someone had started posting weird videos to my channel and then started systematically deleting all of my videos one by one. Within a couple of hours they tried to auction off my channel to the highest bidder, but then decided to just delete my entire channel instead. I was absolutely devastated. It felt like a dream because I was woken up so abruptly; I couldn't help but cry into Ricky's ear for a while until I finally pulled myself together and tried to get my channel back. I quickly discovered that the worst of it was still to come.

It turned out they hadn't just hacked my channel; they had basically hacked my life.

I stayed up all night figuring out the extent of the damage. I tried to get on Twitter, and it wasn't working and I realized they hacked that, too. I was quick to notice this, so it was easy to get back—I changed my password and quickly set up two-step verification and I was back online. When I went to check my email, I couldn't get in. They had changed my password and my security questions. Even when I got someone on the phone, I had no way to verify that I was really me because I didn't even know what my security questions were anymore. Soon a Twitter account proudly proclaimed responsibility for taking down my channel. I sat up all night trying to get my channel back, and while I definitely didn't "follow" them, I did read everything they tweeted.

The hacker had used a program that tracked my keystrokes, so they had my passwords literally to everything. My passwords were all different from one another and were definitely not something that could be easily guessed, so it only made sense that they used a program to get them. I mean, I've never been one to use the obvious passwords like *password* or *1234*. (Seriously, if these are your passwords to anything, put down this book and go change them right now. But, you know, come back, please.) Since they had the passwords to my iCloud and Amazon accounts, they got all kinds of precious information. Everything from my phone number, to my parents' phone numbers, my address, and my credit card number. They even somehow found my dad's address, something I didn't even know by heart—but they had it. And soon they tweeted out a link to a document that contained all of this information and more. We called the police, but because any threats they made were made online and there was no physical threat, they said there was nothing they could really do about it—I sort of felt like they were treating it like it was a joke.

As soon as my information was leaked, almost immediately my phone started to ring. My phone practically exploded from the number of texts. It was mostly fans, but it was completely overwhelming and, because I have fans from all over the world, I was getting texts twenty-four hours a day from a bunch of different countries. My phone was dying constantly. Not only did I get calls on my cell phone, but I also got a ton of calls on my landline. It was literally ringing off the hook. My mom answered the phone a couple of times, and for the most part people hung up because she doesn't sound like me. It got to the point where we couldn't take the constant ringing sound, so we unplugged it and eventually canceled our landline altogether. RIP, home phones.

My mom didn't get any calls on her cell phone because she had recently changed her number. I apologize to whoever had her old one. My dad checked in a lot to see if we were okay. It's one of the only times that my parents actually semi–got along after the divorce, because they were concerned for me and for my safety. But then when people started calling his cell phone, he just got pissed and made me feel like it was my fault, even though it really wasn't.

A couple days later the packages started arriving. I remember I was sitting in my kitchen with my mom and a friend of hers who worked in law enforcement and had dealt with online crime a lot, when the doorbell rang. We all just froze. My mom peered through the window and saw the mailman walking away. Neither of us was expecting a package, but we took it inside and for a while we just stared at it. It was from Amazon, so finally we figured it was safe to open it. Basically the package contained a book about how to train slaves, with a title so offensive that I won't say it out loud, let alone write it in print.

New packages started arriving daily. Some of them were harmless, like astronaut ice cream or a Wii U, but most of them were totally inappropriate. I was only sixteen at the time and someone had sent me a giant purple dildo. In a way I'm weirdly grateful for getting that dildo (WAIT FOR ME TO FINISH THE SENTENCE) because it helped us in three ways. First, when we opened it, we looked at the packing slip and noticed that the credit card used to purchase it was my mom's. We immediately called Amazon and had the charges for all the packages reversed—almost $800 worth of purchases. Then immediately afterward we called the credit card company to cancel the card. Second, for the first time that week my mom and I were able to laugh. I mean, it was a ridiculously huge purple dildo. Seriously, it looked like a giant alien penis. We started to play this game where we would hide it in different places around the house. I put it in the oven once and when my mom opened the oven door to start dinner, she burst out in hysterical laughter.

But the most important reason I am grateful for the dildo (still can't believe that's a sentence) is that once they used our credit card to make purchases, they were officially committing credit card fraud, and it gave us the perfect excuse to get the FBI involved. Internet crime exists in this sort of gray area. What happened to me is called *doxxing*, which is when someone gathers all your personal information and posts it online. In some cases it's not even illegal. It becomes illegal when someone uses the information to threaten someone or steal another person's identity, or when that information is obtained through illegal means, like hacking into someone's private email (which is why that guy who posted all those nude photos of celebrities a couple of years ago is still in jail). The FBI can get permission to access intense privacy data from all the websites my hacker attacked. They figured out that, even though there was only one Twitter account, the "hacker" was actually a group of people, and in order to find them they had to go tweet by tweet and login by login to trace any information the hackers hadn't masked, which took a little while. We kept them updated whenever something happened, and I knew they were working hard.

But even while the FBI was on the case, my life changed for a couple of months. Later that week, someone had three hundred dollars worth of pizza sent to my house. They didn't put a credit card down, so the poor driver showed up expecting we were going to give him cash. We told him to take the pizzas back, that we didn't feel like eating twenty pizzas that night. In the end the expensive pizza delivery was a good thing, because they had to put an email address down for the online order and that helped the FBI track them.

Then people started showing up at my house. Now, you guys know I love you, but it's a little invasive to show up to someone's house that you don't really know. After that, people started driving by my house. You may think I'm just paranoid, but the neighborhood in which I grew up is basically a circle. There is no outlet and it's the kind of small town where you know people's cars. And there were a bunch of new cars driving through our neighborhood and slowing down as they passed my house. The FBI told me I couldn't leave my house through the front door. It pretty much got to the point where I stopped feeling safe in my own home.

I've always had nightmares, but the ones I had during that time period started to feel like real possibilities. In the nightmares I was running around my house trying to lock all the doors and windows because a strange man was outside trying to get in. He was always a step behind, but every time I reached a new lock, three seconds later, there he was. I kept waking up feeling like *What if this really happens? What if I can't get to the lock in time?*

I'll never forget the moment when they wiped my iCloud account. The night I got doxxed, an alert popped up on my phone that read, "If you do not DM this Twitter account in one minute I am going to wipe your iCloud." I stared at the alert trying to figure out what I should do. I knew he was just trying to elicit a response. Before I could even make a decision, my iPhone and iPad went black. I had lost everything: all my pictures, all my texts, all my contacts. I just started to cry.

When all of this was happening, I was too afraid to post anything for a week. No Twitter, no Instagram, and saddest of all, no YouTube videos. After my weeklong disappearance on social media, I finally started tweeting and posting to Instagram again, but I still didn't really feel comfortable posting on my channel for another three weeks. I talked to my mom about quitting YouTube altogether. I was afraid the people who had doxxed me were still watching, and there was nothing stopping them from doing it again. I have always been a super-private person and this was such a huge invasion of privacy, I started to feel like the cons of being a YouTuber were outweighing the pros.

In the end, I kept going, because I didn't want the hackers to win. And they didn't. Thankfully, the FBI tracked the guys and caught them. The experience taught me how to deal when stuff like this happens. You literally have to make reports of everything, because law enforcement won't take it seriously unless they have a buildup of evidence. Unfortunately, getting hacked is something that has happened to a lot of YouTubers.

It's the ugly side of Internet fame.

While it was definitely one of the worst things that ever happened to me, it was certainly not the only time in my life I've had to deal with creepy stuff.

Being doxxed taught me that when bad things happen, the people who step up are the people to keep around. The night I found out, Ricky sat on the phone with me for hours, listening to me complain

1. MARRIAGE LETTER

I love getting letters and artwork from fans. All forms of fan support are awesome, but there's just something nice about getting mail that isn't bills, coupons, or takeout menus. I save fan letters in binders as inspiration. But one time this man from Belgium sent me a twenty-page letter that explained how we were going to get married and detailed out some pretty weird plans for our future. Now, if I got a marriage proposal from a thirteen-year-old with a crush, I might think it was cute. But this guy was in his forties.

2. RANDOM GIRL TWEETING MY PHONE NUMBER

In January of 2014, a girl from my high school posted my phone number on a local Bucks County swim team Twitter account. Within a few hours I had over five hundred texts. Not all of them were mean, and a majority of them came from some kind of spam account that texted me "LOL" over and over from different numbers. But since they weren't all coming from the same number, I couldn't just delete the chat or block the number, so it was the most frustrating thing ever. Because, as I've said before, I'm basically the best Internet detective, I figured out who did it. She wasn't someone I really knew. I did a little digging with the help of my friends back home and found out that she went through a guy from my English class's phone when he wasn't looking and stole my contact info. She did it as a "joke," because she somehow thought posting someone's personal information online would be hilarious. Let me be totally clear: It's not.

3. PAPARAZZI FANS

Sometimes fans will tweet me pictures of myself out in public doing random things like going through security at an airport, shopping at the grocery store, or driving my car. While I have no problem with fans taking pictures, it's sort of funny to see them and think, *Whoa, someone was watching me.* If you see me in the grocery store, just come say hi! I swear I don't bite.

4. PHONE PERVERT

When I got doxxed, a random guy found all of the personal information that was posted online. Before we cut off our landline, this literal pedophile started calling and leaving really lewd and threatening messages for me on our answering machine. My mom never let me listen to them, and to this day she won't tell me what they said, but I was sixteen and apparently they were pervy enough to get him booked as a sex offender.

5. QUESTIONS ABOUT MY PERSONAL LIFE

An uncomfortable number of people ask me questions about my dating life. When I meet a guy I'm really serious about, a guy I think I could marry someday, I promise, you'll meet him. But until then, those are just things I'm not going to talk about for the same reason that when I turn twenty-one I'll never post a drunk video: I have a lot of young fans. Parents will bring their kids to my meet-and-greets and thank me for being a role model. That's always the mind-set I have when I post stuff online. So many people have their eyes on me and I wouldn't want to give anyone a bad impression, especially my family and friends.

6. KNOWING WHERE I LIVE

The summer I graduated from high school, I moved into a house with Andrea Russett, Arden Rose, and Lauren Elizabeth. We only had two rules: no filming in front of the house and no taking pictures in front of the house, because we wanted to keep our address private. However, we didn't consider that maybe "no pictures from the roof" should be a rule, and some of us posted pictures of the view from our amazing roof deck. Within a day, people on Twitter started DMing us pictures of our house. It was really crazy because we had never put our address online anywhere, so someone must have taken the view and reverse engineered the vantage point or something. I don't even know if that's a thing.

7. ALMOST GETTING KICKED OUT OF A HOTEL

Whenever a bunch of YouTubers travels together for an Internet event, it's totally normal to find fans hanging out in the lobby of our hotel or outside the front doors. I'm happy to take pictures with people and say hi. But one time, when I went to London for a DigiFest, fans pushed the boundaries and actually followed us up to our rooms. Anthony and I were trying to film a video, and fans were banging on the door and being so loud we got a noise complaint from the hotel. We went outside to take pictures with them and a few minutes later someone from the hotel came up and told us that if we didn't quiet down we'd actually be kicked out of the hotel. I was so worried about what would happen and where we would sleep if that happened, considering we were in another country and it wasn't even us who were being loud. Thankfully, we didn't get kicked out. I don't think I could've handled sleeping on a park bench.

8. PEOPLE TAKING PICTURES OF ME EATING

In high school, there was this period of time where people would take pictures of me eating lunch at school. I know it's not half as creepy as other things on this list, but it was still totally invasive. They'd post them online like "Hey, look at Jennxpenn eating LOL!" I just didn't get it. We went to the same school, I saw you every single day, there's no need to take creepy pictures of me from afar.

9. OLD MEN BEING MAD ABOUT TROLL-Y VIDEO TITLES

I know I told you your video title should always relate to your video, and it should, but sometimes when I'm pulling a prank I'll put the name of the prank in the title. One time, as part of a truth-or-dare video, I pranked my mom by telling her that there were naked photos of me on the Internet, so I titled the video "Naked Pictures Leaked," and I got all these comments from middle-aged men who were really angry that I had lied about the naked pictures. Seriously? Which one of us should be angry here? The same thing happened when I titled a video "My First Time." For those of you who don't know, "My First Time" is a YouTube tag where you talk about the first time you did a bunch of different things (none of which are sex). However, these same guys got mad and posted angry comments and tweets because they wanted to hear about how I lost my virginity. Again, think about it; if anyone should be mad, I really think it should be me.

10. PEOPLE PRETEND TO *BE* ME ON SOCIAL MEDIA

I think it's awesome when my fans make Tumblrs or Pinterest boards about me. Sometimes they even make Facebook fan pages, Vine edits, or YouTube videos made up of pictures and videos of me. I think my absolute favorite is when my fans make Twitter and Instagram accounts dedicated to me. Any and all kinds of support from my fans make me so happy. But when people create Twitter accounts and Facebook pages where they pretend to *be* me, it's super-creepy.

and letting me cry. It didn't matter that it was 4:00 a.m. and he was probably exhausted. It didn't even matter that there were moments where I wasn't saying anything at all, because my tears wouldn't let me. I needed him and he was there. My mom was by my side every step of the way, trying to shield me from any darkness as best she could. She kept in contact with the FBI so I didn't have to worry. She deleted upsetting voicemails so I'd never have to hear them. She made me feel like it was all going to be okay and never let me know just how terrified she really was. Jordyn and Gabriela were there for me more than I could've ever asked for. They would come pick me up every day for school, drive all the way down the driveway to the back of the house so I could sneak out the back door without being seen, and drive me home after school. They became the ones I could open up to about what was happening, how scared I was, and all my nightmares. A lot of my YouTube friends also stepped up to show me support during that time. For the first time in my life, people had my back.

MY BOYFRIEND, THE INTERNET

I am debatably the most shipped person on YouTube. For those of you who read that and imagined me climbing into a cardboard box filled with packing peanuts and hopping onto a UPS truck, let me explain what *shipping* really means. Shipping is when fans create fictional stories, videos, etc. of two people they'd like to see in a relationship. Shipping is funny, because when you get shipped with someone it creates this weird dynamic where you can't help but think about what dating that person would be like. And sometimes

that feels super-creepy. Some of my guy friends are like brothers to me. Imagine kissing your brother; like, *really* imagine it. Pretty gross.

Well, I hate to break it to you, but I'm not dating any YouTubers. However, I do have a boyfriend and it's pretty serious. We've been together for, like, ever. We started flirting when I was in elementary school. Even when I dated other guys, I was really thinking about him. In high school we decided to make it official, and now we're pretty much married. Most of you guys probably know him pretty well. His name is The Internet.

Technically, I've been online dating since the summer before seventh grade. Okay, not really, but the first time I spoke to my first "boyfriend," Sam, was over AIM. We hadn't actually met in real life, but my friend Tina from my soccer team thought we would like each other, so she set us up.

For our first date, we decided to go to the mall with Tina and another friend from our team, Melissa. It was basically my first date, so I thought, you know, safety in numbers. It was not a life-changing experience. I only remember little bits of it. I remember he was wearing Hollister. I remember we wandered through Aéropostale. I don't remember having an actual conversation. Toward the end of the of the day we took pictures in a photo booth—all four of us—and I remember that for the last picture Melissa and Tina jumped out of the booth, leaving me and Sam alone in the picture. I still have it. We look so awkward.

I dated Sam for two months; by then we were in seventh grade at the same school, but our middle school was split into four different wings and, since we were in different wings, I never really saw him. When I did, I would say hi, but that was it. We mostly just talked on AIM. One day, he came to my house to hang out, and we had our first kiss. It went something like this:

Sam: "So, um, have you ever had your first kiss?"

Me: "Uh, no."

Sam: "Um, so, well, we should kiss."

Me: "Um. Okay. Right now?"

Sam: "Yeah."

For a minute we just sort of stood in the center of my bedroom, facing each other. Neither of us knew what we were doing. Even though we were literally inches apart, it was like we lacked the technology to bridge the gap. I was so nervous. I think I even said out loud, "I'm nervous." Finally, I leaned forward and pecked him on the lips. We didn't discuss the incident for the rest of the day. Or ever. While this sounds like the most awkward thing ever, it wasn't even the most awkward relationship at my school. Once, a girl from my school dumped her boyfriend of several months because a boy passed her in the hall and she thought the back of his head was cute. But as soon as she saw the boy's face, she dumped him, too.

Of course these weren't real relationships; they were essentially an overly complicated way of telling someone you thought they were cute. Because that's all middle school relationships were about. Back then, it was like you dated a boy for a day but you never actually talked to each other. Your friends would negotiate the terms and then for the rest of the day you would be "going out." Then one of your friends would notify the boy's friend that the relationship was over. The whole thing could play out without making any contact.

One of my friends dated a guy for six months without speaking to him. She would get so nervous when she'd see him in the halls that she'd intentionally walk the other way. For her birthday he got her a pair of earrings and gave them to her in front of her locker. That was moving way too fast. She broke up with him soon after.

During sophomore year, I got my first *real* boyfriend, Danny. We met hanging out with a bunch of kids in my friend Veronica's neighborhood. Danny was hot and we liked the same TV shows, but other than that we were pretty different. I've always heard that opposites attract, but I'm not so sure that's true. He got me a necklace for Valentine's Day and I got him hockey tickets, *and* I went to the game with him—which is sort of like two presents, because I hate watching sports. But then, one day I decided I needed to break up with him. Nothing really happened. Danny got weirdly jealous when Tyler Cleary asked me to go to senior prom with him. It was weird for two reasons: First, Tyler went to a different school, so it's not like I was going to prom with Tyler *instead* of Danny, and second—and most important—Tyler is gay. But Danny insisted that I was going to kiss him because it was prom. He didn't seem to get that while I had zero percent interest in kissing Tyler, Tyler had even less interest in kissing me. But that wasn't really it; I kind of just stopped liking him.

Although I had decided I was definitely breaking up with him, I didn't really know how to break up with someone. I knew we were definitely past the stage where my friend could just tell his friend we were done. I knew I couldn't just text him, either. But the idea of actually facing him made me feel like I might actually vomit. So I called him on the phone. When he answered, I had no idea what to say, so I used every cliché a person has ever used while breaking up with someone. I told him I needed to focus on myself. I told him we were better as friends. I didn't exactly say, "It's not you; it's me," but, basically, yeah, that's what I said.

He took it really poorly. He texted me saying he was coming over to win me back. I texted him that I wasn't home, but that was a total lie. I was just scared. What were we going to talk about? What was he going to say? I had already made up my mind. I figured I had a few minutes to formulate a plan. Neither of us could drive yet, so I'd have at least a bike-ride length of time to figure out what I was going to do. But he got to my house in record time—his mom drove him. I called my mom, freaking out, and she assured me that I didn't have to talk to him if I didn't want to. Now, in retrospect, I think she meant that I could calmly tell him our breakup wasn't up for discussion. I took it a different way. I turned off the lights in my house and pretended not to be home. I watched his mom waiting in the car for her son to return from his mission. I listened to him repeatedly ring the doorbell until he finally gave up, got back in his mom's car, and went home.

I realize this story makes me sound low-key terrible, so just for the record, Danny landed on his feet. He got a new girlfriend right away and they're still together today. But at the time, she absolutely hated me. At one point she actually threatened to physically fight me, which doesn't make any sense, because I was over him. He was all hers. Still, I feel really bad about the way I handled breaking up with Danny. I've always been the worst at dealing with guys. I used all of those clichés because, honestly, I thought the truth sounded even more made-up.

The truth was, at fifteen, I was breaking up with my boyfriend to focus on my career.

Adults break up with people to focus on their careers all the time, but doing it at fifteen felt weird. Sophomore year had been kind of a tipping point for me when I decided to take making YouTube videos more seriously. But even at fifteen, I knew it was going to take a lot of work and I was going to have to sacrifice other things in my life to do it.

The first thing I gave up was extracurricular activities—that happened in ninth grade. When I was younger I was really into sports, especially soccer. I wasn't trying to be the next Mia Hamm, but I took it seriously and I was pretty good. However, I was bad at time management. Between making videos, school, and soccer, I had no time to begin with, and I spent a lot of the time I did have procrastinating. When it came time for homework, I'd run out the clock by checking Twitter, watching YouTube videos, and checking Twitter again. Most of the time I'd still get it all done (though *how* is still sort of a mystery to me). But sometimes, getting my homework done meant I didn't have time to make and edit a video, and my subscribers noticed. Some people would leave disappointed comments, but for the most part people would just say, "Oh, it's okay." I still felt bad.

Once I hit high school, my homework basically tripled. I was always sort of into school, so I was in all honors and AP classes. I knew I wouldn't have enough time for soccer, school, and YouTube—something had to go. I wasn't going to stop making videos and it's not like dropping out of school was an option (or at least not a legal option), so I said good-bye to extracurriculars. There was this brief period in junior year when I was freaking out about college applications and I tried to pick them up again. I joined all kinds of clubs, like Future Business Leaders of America and Volunteers for Community Service. I even signed up to manage the track team, but that was a total disaster. By then I was traveling so much for work that I was never around. I was the worst track team manager in history; I didn't actually manage anything, nor did I go to a single meet. Basically, all I did was wear the team sweatshirt. (I still have it; it's super-comfortable.)

In the middle of sophomore year, with the encouragement of Mr. Hentz, and almost 100,000 subscribers, I decided to treat making YouTube videos as a job. So I decided to set a schedule for when I uploaded a video. I had always kind of tried to post videos on Saturdays, but sophomore year is when I actually made it a thing. With school and homework, it was hard to get a video ready to upload during the week. At this point I was working hard on improving the quality of my videos, which meant more time prepping, shooting, and editing. In order to make sure I could always get a video done, I had to cut something else out of my life. My Friday nights.

So while you guys were hanging out with your friends or going to a rager at some kid's house while their parents were out of town, I was most likely home, in my room, by myself, finishing my videos. Sophomore year there were definitely times when I felt like I missed out on something cool. I'd get a text from Veronica or Hailey telling me what they were up to, or see pictures of them hanging out on Facebook, and I'd get the slightest twinge of jealousy. But you know what? I could not name what a single one of those things was now. So if you're a sophomore sitting at home on a Friday night thinking everyone is doing something better than you, don't worry about it. Chances are, they probably aren't. And even if they are, in two years it won't matter. For me, staying in on Friday nights was totally worth it; by the end of the school year I started working with AwesomenessTV.

During my junior year of high school I started traveling for work. In October, AwesomenessTV flew me to LA to film a collab with Lia Marie Johnson. Lia liked my videos, and when she found out I was also working with AwesomenessTV, she asked them if they would help us film a video together. I was there for six days and we filmed a bunch of videos, including a guide to Halloween, a couple episodes of *Terry the Tomboy* (Lia's show on their channel), and a video for my channel called "Caught in the Forest." I'd filmed collabs before, but filming a collab with a network was a totally different experience. I'd never filmed in a studio and I'd definitely never had a crew—unless you count making one of my friends hold my camera.

By March, I was traveling at least once a month for work. I had started working with Teen.com doing *Stranger Danger,* which gave me even more opportunities to fly to LA to film videos. My first trip with Teen.com was for five days in March to shoot promos for my show. While I was there, I filmed a blindfolded hairstyling challenge with Meghan Camarena and hung out with some of my other friends who lived in LA. By then I was also traveling for Internet events: My channel had gotten big enough that I was actually invited to Playlist Live and DigiFest NYC as a professional. In June, I filmed one of my first branded videos, for Universal Studios' *Despicable Me 2.* They flew me to Universal Studios Florida for a screening of the movie and gave me an all-access

pass to the theme park—and all I had to do was post a video about my experience. Traveling is literally one of my favorite things, and I loved getting to film collabs and spend time with my YouTube friends. But it meant I once again had to give something else up in order to travel: school.

I've always been a school nerd. I mean, I was never one of those super-competitive nerds who asks what everyone else got on tests just so they can say they did the best. But I always worked hard and wanted to do well. The thing is, it's really hard to do well in school when you're not there. Every time I had to travel, I missed two to five days of school. I must have missed forty or fifty days total of school in my junior year. Technically, you're considered truant after twenty, but my guidance counselor worked it out because I was missing school for my job. My teachers were all very supportive. They would give me all the assignments I'd miss when I was working and I would do my best to do them on my own. But it turns out that all those things your teacher says in class while you're napping or passing notes or texting under the table are actually really important. Sometimes I struggled with assignments because I had no idea what was going on in class.

I love science, so in my junior year I took both anatomy and microbiology. My anatomy teacher was great; he was one of those teachers who throws all the notes up on the board and does dynamic presentations with intricate models to make sure people really understand how the body works. He was a really nice guy, too. He respected what I was doing, so he'd take it easy on me when I'd miss class. But I was still missing the *class* part. I'd have to do these assignments with just my textbook, which is pretty difficult when you're learning about every inch of the human body. I remember we had this test where we had to walk around and label models of different organs and I hadn't seen half of them before. Somehow it was hard to translate the pictures in the book with the 3-D model version. And to some degree, that's what happened in all my classes.

I felt disconnected, because I'd come back from missing a few days of school and we'd be on a whole new chapter. I was just one kid, so it's not like they would say, "Before we start this lesson, we're going to tell Jenn what's she's missed." I know you're probably thinking that I was lucky that I got to ditch class and basically get away with it, but while I hated high school, one of my favorite parts of it was the actual *school* part. I know that sounds super-dorky, but I like learning. It's also the only part of high school that is important after you leave. The second you get into the real world, no one cares whether you were popular when you were sixteen. They do care whether or not you're smart.

The main thing I had to give up happened even before I went to high school.

I had to give up the idea that I would ever fit in.

Even when people stopped picking on me, people still wanted things from me. And after what happened with Veronica, it was hard to figure out whom I could trust. I just wanted to be treated like everyone else, but it was clear that was never going to happen. My videos made me stand out. When I'd walk down the

TOP 10 THINGS NOBODY WILL CARE ABOUT WHEN YOU LEAVE HIGH SCHOOL

1. POPULARITY

I get it: When you're in high school, popularity means something. It's sort of like money. It buys you a ton of friends, access to cooler parties, a hotter boyfriend, and a way better table in the cafeteria. But if you're in high school and you're super-popular, you should probably spend that imaginary cash now because it's not really worth anything once you graduate. Leaving high school hits a sort of reset button. I've made a ton of friends since leaving high school and not one of them has ever said, "Hey, were you popular in high school? Oh, you weren't. I can't be friends with you."

2. DRAMA

When you leave high school, you realize all that drama that seemed so important is just really exhausting. When you're in high school, everyone totally feeds off of drama. A stupid disagreement between two friends that could be solved if they just sat down and had a conversation turns into some super-dramatic school-wide war. People talk shit about each other and spill secrets and take sides in fights that have nothing to do with them. Do you know what people do once they leave high school? They sit down and have the conversation. Unless they're on a reality TV show—then they throw drinks or something.

3. PROM - RELATED STRESS

I don't know why, but it seems like every year proms get to be a bigger and bigger deal. Asking someone to prom has become sort of like proposing. It's not enough to just ask; you have to, like, *do* something. One guy had the principal ask his date for him. Another guy did it over the school's intercom system. This senior I was sort-of dating my junior year asked me to his prom by standing in the middle of the hallway holding up a sign. I was super-embarrassed. But once the asking's done, there's still the dress and the hair. And figuring out which friends go in what limo becomes like a giant game of musical chairs. It's months of stress and planning for one night you may or may not remember in five years. If you don't go to prom with the guy that you've loved since freshman year, or even if you miss it entirely, remember: it's just a school dance.

4. WHETHER OR NOT YOU HAD A BOYFRIEND

It sucks to feel like you're the only one who doesn't have a boyfriend. But not having a boyfriend in high school doesn't mean you won't have a boyfriend in college or when you're an adult. Besides, even if you did have a boyfriend in high school, your new boyfriend really doesn't want to hear about him.

5. THE TIME YOU DIDN'T MAKE THE JV BASKETBALL TEAM

Unless you're trying to play a sport in college or become a professional athlete or something, no one cares that you didn't make your high school team. In fact, no one cares if you did.

6. WHAT CAR YOU DROVE

I lived in the kind of town where kids got cars for their sixteenth birthdays. And they didn't get just any cars; they got nice cars, a lot of white BMWs. I didn't get a car when I turned sixteen. I saved up money I earned from my channel and bought my mom's old car. It's nothing fancy. It is white, but it's definitely not a BMW, and it still works just fine.

7. THAT TIME YOU FELL AND GOT PUDDING EVERYWHERE

Throughout my high school career, I had a lot of embarrassing things happen to me. Although I tend to erase most of them from my memory, a few of them stick. On the first day of junior year, my friend and I decided to carpool to school. Junior year is the first year everyone drives themselves to school, so we were feeling like total badasses. But as I was walking to her car, a bee stung me. I started freaking out and jumping around and screaming, but she couldn't see the bee from her car window so, to her, I just looked like a total psycho. And I guess I'm, like, slightly allergic to bees, because on the way to school my sting started swelling. So instead of walking into school like a badass, I had to run to the nurse's office. But something kind of cool happens when you leave high school. These experiences that were totally mortifying sort of lose their power. They just become funny stories.

8. WHAT WAS COOL WHEN YOU WERE IN HIGH SCHOOL

Remember how I said that when I got to middle school, everyone thought Hollister, Abercrombie, and Aéropostale were really cool? Remember how I told you not to worry about it? Here's why: By the time I got to high school, the same people who had made fun of kids who didn't wear Hollister or Abercrombie or Aéropostale started making fun of the kids who still did. Literally the same things that made people "cool" in middle school made them "losers" in high school. Again, I don't know who decides these things. Maybe there's some sort of secret committee or something. At some point almost anything everyone thought was cool just stops being cool. I used to think planking was really cool, but now I have no idea why. In all seriousness, the only thing that is consistently cool is not caring about what other people think is cool.

9. WHERE YOU SAT IN THE CAFETERIA

My high school's cafeteria was totally the cafeteria from *Mean Girls*. Sitting at a certain table meant you were a certain kind of person. And people would sometimes pretend to be something they weren't just to get to a "better" table. The reality is, the only people who even know where you sat in the cafeteria are the people who went to your high school. And when you graduate you won't see most of them again (unless you're a creepy Facebook stalker). If you're lucky, you'll keep in touch with a few close friends who accept you for who you actually are. Find those people. Sit with them.

10. HIGH SCHOOL

Like all of it. Except grades.

halls, people would make jokes like "Oh my god, you're here!" and "Wow, you're so famous." While the jokes weren't super-mean, they didn't exactly make me happy to be there. But by March of junior year it didn't really matter anymore; I was traveling so much for work that I felt totally disconnected from school and just stopped caring what people there thought of me.

In the beginning, even though I was there for work, trips to LA felt like a vacation from my real life. Any chance to see my YouTube friends was a really big deal. But then something shifted—YouTube started to feel like my real life. Between filming in LA and Playlist in Orlando, seeing my YouTube friends stopped feeling like a big deal and just started to feel normal. They stopped being my "YouTube friends" and just became my real friends. Even in April, when I had a weekend free, I chose to go to New York with Jack Baran to see Alexa Losey and our other beauty guru friends at IMATS, the International Make-up

Artist Trade Show. Even though we were in New York and going to a giant convention center filled with thousands of people, mostly it just felt like I was hanging out with my friends, the way any other teenager would on the weekends.

Even though I missed a lot of normal high school experiences, like formals, proms, and going to school five days in a row, I got to experience my own thing. And for that reason alone, I don't have any regrets. There were moments when it was hard not feeling normal. But the sacrifices were worth it because they brought me to where I am today. Right now I'm living in my dream city, working every day doing something that I love. I'm constantly like, "Oh my god. This is my life." There are just some things in life more important than being like everyone else or having a boyfriend.

Now, I'm not saying I haven't dated any guys since sophomore year; I have, just never seriously. I do date occasionally, but when it comes to serious relationships, I just really don't have time. It's not that I'm, like, indifferent to guys; I'm actually sort of a hopeless romantic. But when I start liking a guy, I think about him a lot and it gets kind of distracting. It's hard to get a video done when I'm thinking about ways I can start a conversation with a guy, finding excuses to text him, imagining ways I could ask him to hang out without him thinking that I like him. You know—normal girl stuff. When relationships end, the whole thing gets even worse. I just want to lie in bed and think about why things didn't work out. I replay moments wondering whether things would've worked out if I had just done something different or said something different. I think we all do that. It's normal to want to try to figure out what went wrong. But the reality is, I don't have time for that because I have a responsibility to my subscribers. I can't just say,

No new video this week; I'm sad about boys.

I do want to be in a serious relationship someday, but for now—and this sounds sort of terrible—in order for me to want to make time for a relationship with a guy, he has to be at least as good as The Internet. And most aren't. Especially not the ones I seem to like. I don't know why, but I tend to gravitate toward, well, assholes. It's slightly out of control. You know the kind of guy who treats you differently when you're alone than when you're with a group of people? The kind who ignores your texts for a few days, then shows up like nothing happened? Yup. Those guys are for me. I once dated a guy who was nice and I found it confusing. He'd open a door or pull out a chair—the whole chivalrous thing—and I'd be like, "What are you doing?" In the end, I decided he was "too nice," which, by the way, isn't a real thing. So while I figure out how to stop liking assholes, I think I'll stick with my current boyfriend, The Internet. He's been super-good to me so far.

DECISIONS

ARE

HARD

Decisions are hard. I have never been the most decisive person. As a kid, I was a big fan of flipping a coin. Even now I still have trouble making really basic decisions. Like food. My house is near so many great takeout places that I'm paralyzed by choice. Sometimes I'll literally call my mom and ask her what I should eat even though she lives across the country. It gets even worse if I'm eating with Lauren Elizabeth because, like me, Lauren suffers from food indecision. We can never decide what to eat, and it's so bad that sometimes we'll just get in the car and start driving with no destination, just to get the process going. I also have trouble deciding what to put on top ten lists. I've had to make a bunch of top ten lists for my show on AwesomenessTV, *Jennxpenn's Top 10's* (and now for this book), but so often I have trouble coming up with ten things to fit a category. Sometimes I wish my name rhymed with *five*.

I've had to make some actual tough decisions in my life, but the toughest was deciding whether or not to move to LA for my senior year.

I've always thought it would be cool to spend the summer in LA, but it never seemed like a real possibility until I talked to Andrea Russett at Playlist Live. She was already doing online school and had decided to make the jump permanently, and she needed a roommate. A lot of my YouTube friends were already out there or had plans to head out there, so I wasn't worried about having to make new friends.

Work-wise, it just made sense. If I stayed at home for the summer, I was going to have to fly to LA basically every other week to film the rest of my *Stranger Danger* videos for Teen.com and videos for AwesomenessTV. And it's summer; it's not like I'd be missing any classes. My mom was pretty supportive. I wasn't the kind of kid who got into trouble for no reason, so she knew she could totally trust me. I'd also been working with AwesomenessTV for over a year at this point, and my mom had gotten close with the people safer knowing I had some solid adults in my life I could turn to if my car flamed ... my finger in a freak cooking accident. Besides, it was just for the summer.

That really was the plan—just for the summer. The thought that I might stay in LA hadn't even occurred to me yet. I planned to move there after graduation, but at this point there was no question that I was moving back home in September for my senior year. Andrea and I were subletting an apartment in Westwood from UCLA students who would be back to reclaim it once school started, so we needed to get out in September anyway. We made a deal with a company to ship my car across the country in July and ship it back in September—it was a packaged deal: there and back. And I really only brought enough stuff for two months.

At that time, I couldn't imagine living on my own at sixteen; I was nervous about being away from home for even two months. Being away from home had never been my strong suit. I was the kid at sleepovers who almost always had to go home early. Don't get me wrong: Sleepovers are super-fun. I loved making prank phone calls, eating junk food, and watching *Mean Girls* for the millionth time. Most of the time I'd be totally fine, but sometimes I'd be hit with a wave of anxiety and I'd need to get home. We'd hit lights-out and I'd just lie there, wide-awake, thinking of ways I could get my mom to pick me up.

In middle school, when my anxiety was at its worst, I didn't want to go to school. Sometimes I would even pretend to be sick at school so I could go home early. I had this down to a science: I would say I had a migraine, because it's something that can't be tested with the equipment available in a school nurse's office. The nurse would let me lie down, and after a half hour she would ask, "Is it better or worse?" I would always say it was "the same," and she would send me home. My mom knew I wasn't sick. She knew it was anxiety-related. But as long as my grades didn't suffer, she would play along.

I never knew when the away-from-home anxiety would pop up. It wasn't like I'd go into the experience thinking, *Yup, it's going to happen this time; I'm going to get nervous and have to go home.* The summer after eighth grade, my friend Micaela Romei from FiveFreshTubers invited me on vacation with her family in Martha's Vineyard. The island is an incredibly beautiful place with this small, old-school beach town vibe. We were staying on her family's boat right on the water. If we wanted to go swimming in the ocean, all we had to do was jump off the side of the boat. I am such a beach person, so this experience was particularly awesome for me, and it was nice to get to spend so much time with one of my YouTube friends. I made it through the whole trip without feeling the gut-wrenching feeling of needing to go home.

When she invited me back the summer after freshman year, I was so pumped. Clearly, I'd had a blast the summer before, why would the second time be any different? For a while, it wasn't: We jumped off boats, went to a camp where we did all kinds of water activities, and I got to hang out with Micaela. We were supposed to be there for two weeks—but about a week in, my anxiety just sort of crept up on me. I secretly texted my mom and told her I needed to come home. My mom understood and covered for me by saying there was a "family emergency." Then she drove all the way from Pennsylvania to Massachusetts, and took the ferry over to the island to pick me up and take me home. (If I haven't said it before: I have the best mom ever.)

On the drive home, my anxiety subsided and I regretted leaving. And that's how it usually went. As soon as I was out of the situation that was making me uncomfortable, I'd realize it wasn't that big of a deal. My anxiety about being away from home faded a bit through high school, because I was traveling so much for work that it just got easier to be away. But on most of those trips my mom came with me. You can't see her in most of my vlogs or Instagram posts from my trips because she hates being on camera. She's only done a video with me, like, once. I was a little embarrassed to have my mom with me because basically all of my friends were older than me, but she was always great about giving me space. (Again: best mom ever.) But more than anything, I was relieved she was there, because I never had to worry about getting that homesick feeling.

By March of junior year I started traveling by myself without getting homesick. Most of the time, I wasn't even worried about it. I had made so many YouTube friends that I knew I'd always have someone with me. Meghan Camarena had become like a big sister to me, so staying at her apartment in LA felt like staying with family. Still, those solo trips were only for a couple days at a time, and now I was going to spend the whole summer in LA. I wanted to believe that my nerves wouldn't get to me, but in the back of my mind the thought lingered: *What if I need to go home?* I tried to push those thoughts out of my head, in case thinking about being homesick would make me homesick.

I arrived in LA on July 5, 2013. My mom flew with me and stayed for a few days to help me get set up, but then she had to head back to Pennsylvania for work. Andrea wasn't arriving for another week, so I spent my first nights in LA alone. It was . . . terrifying. Have you ever noticed that sounds you never really paid attention to during the day suddenly get really loud at night? Like creaking floorboards or rustling trees or a faucet dripping? When you live with other people you can write those noises off as something they're doing. That creaky floorboard sound is my mom getting an extra blanket from the closet. That tree-rustling sound is my roommate opening her window. That leaky faucet is, well, a leaky faucet.

When I'm alone and there's no one to blame for those noises, my mind can go to some pretty creepy places. Is that creaky floorboard the sound of a serial killer opening my front door? Is that rustling the sound of his feet shuffling across my carpet? Is that leaking faucet the countdown clock of a mega-bomb set to destroy the planet? Okay, maybe not that last one. But it can get pretty scary. That's what my first night alone in my apartment was like. I didn't really know what to do, so I just shut my door, locked myself in my room, and pretended that there was someone else in the next room who could account for all the noise. I realize that sleeping in a totally safe apartment in a totally safe part of Los Angeles near a college where there's, like, a ton of security doesn't sound like that big a deal. But for a girl who used to go home from sleepovers, it was an enormous personal victory.

I did get homesick a few times over the course of the summer, but it wasn't serious. I was a little sad to be spending my birthday away from home for the first time, but my friends made it way easier.

Ricky Dillon, Connor Franta, and Jc Caylen took me to In-N-Out, which is a family-owned fast food chain that serves the best burgers in the known universe (well, for fast food), the night before my birthday. After we ate our delicious burgers, July 8 turned into July 9 and the boys sang "Happy Birthday" to me really loudly in front of the entire restaurant. I spent my seventeenth birthday with Meghan, her brother David (we share the same birthday), and a few others at Six Flags Magic Mountain, and Jordyn sent me cupcakes, so it was a pretty great birthday in the end. Sometimes I would see what my friends back home were doing on Facebook or Instagram and it made me miss them and Pennsylvania, but it would pass.

Summer is always fun. No homework. No school. No teachers who somehow always smell like onions. But at home in Pennsylvania there wasn't a whole lot to do, because my town is pretty small. To put it in perspective, I had to drive a half hour to get to the nearest Chipotle. I'd spend most of my time either making YouTube videos or watching YouTube videos. Sometimes my friends and I would hang out by a pool or at one another's houses, but that was about the extent of it. By contrast, LA had never-ending things to do. Alexa Losey had shown me around a little during those times when I had flown out to film videos. But I couldn't believe how much more there was to see. Just walking outside my apartment, I saw more restaurants and clothing stores than there were in my entire hometown. That summer, my friends and I explored LA like it was our own personal playground.

Beyond getting to hang out with my YouTube friends, living in LA created new opportunities for my career. I had so much more time to devote to making videos and editing them just the way I wanted. It helped a lot that literally all my friends in LA were YouTubers, so everyone around me was making videos, too. Being surrounded by people who are all working toward the same sort of goal is the best motivation. I still shot and edited my videos by myself, but if I needed help, it was right there. I could borrow lenses or extra lights from friends if I needed to. YouTube had always been a community, and I'd often talk to my friends about my video ideas. But it's a totally different experience talking to someone about a video idea over iChat compared to talking in person, where he or she can actually help you make the video.

Living in LA also made it way easier to shoot videos for AwesomenessTV. Instead of packing a suitcase, getting together all my homework for the week, driving to the airport, watching the TSA screen my tiny bottle of face wash to make sure it wasn't an explosive, sitting on a plane for six hours, and then shooting a video, I could just hop in my car and be there in less than ten minutes. Although sometimes, the videos were a bit torturous, like the tin can challenge I filmed with Lia Marie Johnson. We drew numbers out of a hat and had to eat from an unmarked can with the corresponding number. Somehow, Lia got all the fruit and I got all the animal food. Have you ever wondered what cat food tastes like? Stop. It tastes terrible; like, worse than you can ever imagine.

I also got to shoot some sketches with AwesomenessTV. I hadn't previously done a lot of acting, so it was really cool to get that opportunity. And because I didn't have to then hop back on a plane the next day, I could shoot even more videos, so AwesomenessTV gave me the chance to create my own show.

TOP 10 BEST PARTS OF MY BEST SUMMER EVER

1. LIVING NEAR MY YOUTUBE FRIENDS

By total coincidence, the apartment I shared with Andrea was right down the street from the apartment Connor and Ricky moved into that summer. The two of them had also decided to head to LA for the summer and had gotten a one-bedroom apartment that had two beds. Jc decided to jump on board, and all three of them road-tripped across the country. To be clear, that's three guys in probably the tiniest one-bedroom apartment you could imagine. To make it a little crazier, Kian Lawley decided he was going to move up from San Clemente, a town a couple hours south of LA. Jc and Kian had to sleep on the couches, and while I still think they were totally insane for packing that many guys into that small apartment, it was a blast to have them so close for my first few weeks in LA. By August, they'd moved into a house about twenty minutes away, but it had a pool, so it became kind of a home base for all of us to hang out.

2. RANDOMLY RUNNING INTO MY YOUTUBE FRIENDS

Before I moved to LA for that summer, I'd really only see my YouTube friends at a YouTube event like VidCon or Playlist Live. Any other time, we'd have to make a special plan, and usually that involved someone getting on a plane or taking a long train ride. But in LA, I could just bump into them randomly. This would mostly happen at The Grove, which is this cool outdoor mall set up to look like a sort of small town with a farmers' market and a trolley running through it.

3. FIESTAS

Usually, summertime means barbecues, but since Jc makes amazing Mexican food, instead of barbecues we'd have fiestas. We'd all meet up at one of our places and make a bunch of Mexican food and just hang out. I learned how to make killer salsa. (The secret is throwing away the jar before anyone knows it's not homemade.)

4. GO-KART RACING, BOWLING, AND MORE

We were always doing something that summer, whether it was seeing a movie, going to Crave Cafe at 1:00 a.m., or going bowling, and it was always a blast. One time, for Jc's birthday, a bunch of us went indoor go-kart racing at this place in Burbank. I'm not much of a risk-taker, for fear of hurting myself, so I'm pretty sure I came in last place every time. It was super-fun, but not worth dying for.

5. PRANK WAR

One time, Andrea and I hosted one of the fiestas, and the boys left us to clean up all the dirty dishes. We started a prank war and got back at them by breaking into their house and covering the whole thing with Silly String. They were so angry and I felt bad and helped them clean it all up, but it was *so* funny and definitely worth it.

6. DRIVING TO THE HOLLYWOOD SIGN

The Hollywood Sign is probably one of the most iconic sights in LA, and one day Andrea and I spontaneously decided that we needed to see it up close. To get there, we had to drive up this scary narrow and curvy road and climb out onto a cliff. We didn't get close enough to touch it, but we got close enough to take a pretty awesome picture.

7. PENNY BOARDING

LA is full of cool outdoor spaces, like the Venice Beach Boardwalk: a crazy beachside walk with freaky street performers, hippie artists, a ton of cool graffiti, and, like, a million places to buy sunglasses for five dollars. That summer we all bought penny boards, which are like mini plastic skateboards, and we used them to cruise around different parts of LA. We didn't walk anywhere. One time, we decided to take our penny boards to Santa Monica and skate down the bike path—but within ten minutes of getting there, Andrea fell down and badly scraped her knee, so we all had to go home. Even though they were super-fun, I think we all had our fair share of falling off of them . . . I know I have.

8. CONCERTS

We had the chance to go to a bunch of cool concerts that summer, but the most iconic show we saw was One Direction. For Rebecca Black's birthday, her parents rented us a party bus and a private box to see One Direction at the Staples Center. A bunch of our fans were in the audience—they saw us in the box and started cheering for us (not even half as loud as they screamed for One Direction, obviously). We even got mobbed as we were trying to leave, so security had to hold us inside until everyone else had left. It was a crazy-cool experience.

9. SPONTANEOUS BEACH DAYS

There were a lot of beach days that summer. I've always been a beach person, but to get to the beach from where I grew up you'd have to drive about two hours. When you live in LA, the beach is practically in your backyard. There were so many times when we'd spontaneously decide to spend the day lying in the sun and swimming in the ocean.

10. VLOGGING

When I vlogged at home, I was always the weird girl carrying around a camera in public. But in LA, everyone's doing their own crazy thing and nobody really cares, so there'd always be, like, three of us vlogging at the same time. It was nice to be in a place where people didn't judge me, with a group of friends who understood exactly what I like to do.

Together with some of the people at AwesomenessTV, we came up with the idea for *Jennxpenn's Top 10's*. I thought a list show would be fun, because there's an endless amount of possibilities when it comes to making lists. The show would also give me a chance to address topics that were really relatable, like annoying things parents do, or the types of things girls hate about guys. I also thought a list show fit in well with the style I'd created on my channel—a mix of me just talking to the camera and sketches. I had filmed videos in the studio before,

T10 - LIES YOU TELL PARENTS
1. I already did my homework
2. I cleaned my room
3. I got an A on the test
4. There's no test tomorrow!
5. There's no school today
6. I went to sleep early last night
7. My homework's on the computer
8. I don't feel good
9. Everyone else's parents said yes!
10. I never lie to you

T10 - WAYS TO SURVIVE EXAMS
1. Write out a schedule of when to study
2. Use study techniques (flashcards)
3. Study with a friend
4. Take breaks
5. Listen to music while studying
6. Reward yourself with candy
7. Get a lot of sleep
8. Bribe your teacher for a good grade
9. Eat a healthy breakfast the morning of
10. Don't study

T10 - PRANKS TO PULL AT SCHOOL
1. Change seats every time the teacher's not looking
2. Laugh loudly at everything the teacher says
3. Bring a pillow and blanket to sleep
4. Unplug the teacher's mouse
5. Hide all the markers in the room
6. Switch names w/ friend
7. Glue a pencil to the ground
8. Pretend you can't hear
9. Ask too many questions
10. Paper airplanes

T10 - THINGS I HATE ABOUT TRAVELING
1. OVERPRICED SNACKS
2. Flight delays
3. Uncomfortable chairs (plane)
4. Sitting next to smelly strangers
5. Strangers sleeping on you
6. TSA
7. Extremely long flights
8. Having the middle seat
9. Airplane meals
10. No wifi on flights

but it was cool to work with a green screen and have a crew there to help create the show.

As summer came to a close, instead of having anxiety about being away from home, I had anxiety about going back. As September crept up on me, I thought more and more about how I loved what I was doing in LA and didn't love the idea of going back to a place where the people around me seemed to kill my creativity. I talked to my mom every day on the phone, slowly starting to drop hints that I didn't want to come back, and she slowly picked them up. I don't think I'll ever forget when my mom called me one day and said, "You want to stay there, don't you?"

We decided that I would stay until my sublet was up, which was September 17, instead of coming back for the first day of school. I would take the first two weeks off from school while we weighed my options. We talked about the things I would be giving up if I stayed. I'd be giving up classes I was really excited about. I had finished most of my required coursework, so most of the courses I would be taking senior year were things I had actually chosen. I would miss all the perks of being a senior, like senior prom and the senior trip. I'd be far away from Gabriela, Jordyn, and the rest of my friends. And even if I did online school, I'd miss having a real high school graduation.

I'd also have to be an adult before I was actually an adult, and I knew that came with a lot of responsibilities I wasn't sure I was ready for.

We also talked about the things I'd be giving up if I left. Staying in LA was really good for my career. Being in LA made it really easy for me to film collabs with other YouTubers for my channel and take opportunities that I could only get if I was out here. One of the first collabs I did out here was a Roommate Tag called "Meet My Roommate" with Andrea. The video is super-funny to rewatch now, because we had only been roommates for, like, a day when we filmed it, so we didn't really know each other that well yet. More collabs followed; they were fun to make and a great way to grow both my channel and the channel of the person I was filming with. My channel grew immensely that summer: Once it was time to leave LA and go back to school, I had reached over 400,000 subscribers. It took me almost four years to get my first 150,000 subscribers. And I gained almost that many again in two months.

If I left, I'd also be giving up the opportunity to start *The Jenn & Andrea Show*. Andrea had helped me with the first couple episodes of *Jennxpenn's Top 10's*, and it was so much fun filming with her. We literally couldn't stop laughing the entire time. We were always joking that we should have our own reality show, and by the end of the summer, what had started as a total joke turned into a real possibility thanks to AwesomenessTV. But the whole hook of the show was the crazy things Andrea and I did as roommates living in LA. Which—obviously—required me to stay in LA. I started to think that going back home would mean taking a step backward in my career.

The reality is, even though you can make YouTube videos from anywhere in the world, YouTubers looking to take their careers to the next level need to be in a place like LA or London. There are a few exceptions, but even they commute to LA for opportunities. Although YouTube lives online, it works largely in Los Angeles. YouTube opened its first production space in LA in 2012, which meant YouTubers had a physical place where they could produce content. The major YouTube networks, like AwesomenessTV, Fullscreen, Maker, and others are all out here. Management companies, agencies, and anything else you can think of having to do with YouTube or the film industry are centered in LA. For European YouTubers, London is the hub for similar reasons. Besides all of that, YouTubers tend to move out here because other YouTubers are out here. That may shift, since YouTube opened another space in New York last year—but for now, LA is the place to be.

Still, there is a sense in the YouTube fan community that moving to LA is a form of "selling out." A sense that, upon arrival, YouTubers stop being themselves and become "so LA," which I don't think is true. But there are some things that are "so LA." Like wearing workout clothes when you're not working out, seeing celebrities in their natural habitat, complaining about traffic, or eating kale. I didn't know vegetables could be trendy, but in LA, basically nothing is cooler than kale. They put it in everything: salads, pastas, even juice. When I first moved out here for the summer, I got comments on my videos that I was becoming "so LA." But the truth is, when I moved out here I didn't become "so LA"—I became more myself.

I think a lot of people hailed the shift in my clothing style as a sign of me changing myself to fit LA. I brought my clothes from back home because that's all I had, but I low-key hated everything in my wardrobe. The truth is, I didn't change the way I dressed to fit LA; I had suppressed my style to be more Pennsylvania. The second I got to LA, I started exchanging my old clothes for the kinds of clothes I actually liked to wear. I was growing up and finding myself at the same time. I remember thinking in high school that Doc Martens were really cool. I bought a pair and wore them to school once, and people commented about how ugly they were. At my school, everyone basically dressed the same, and since I already stuck out more than I wanted to, I followed suit. In LA, I feel more freedom. More freedom of what I like to do and what I like to wear. None of my friends dress exactly the same, and that's okay. It gives me the freedom to explore what I actually like. Which—it turns out—is a lot of dark clothing and chunky boots.

A big reason I wanted to move out here was that I felt comfortable being myself. By junior year, Jordyn, Gabriela, and my YouTube friends helped me accept that it was better to be me than to fit in, but I was never exactly comfortable at school. When I was deciding whether or not to stay in LA, I realized that, outside of Jordyn and Gabriela, mostly all of my friends had been seniors from my upper-level classes, and they weren't going to be there anymore because they'd graduated. All that was left for me in those halls were the Ghosts of Best Friends Past, and the memories of assholes trying to tear me down. In LA I fit in, not because I'm like everyone else, but because everyone accepts me as I am.

My YouTube community in LA made me feel like I had a family even 3,000 miles from home.

When I called my mom to tell her I'd decided to stay in LA she was upset, but she was prepared. She knew what I was going to do even before I did. My mom always knows. I remember one time it was late in LA and I was upset, and she called me at two in the morning her time and said, "I had a feeling something was wrong so I just wanted to see if you were okay." I swear she has a sixth sense about me. She decided to withdraw me from school so that if I changed my mind I could come home and reenroll myself. My mom has always been my biggest supporter. We promised we'd see each other all the time, and we still try to fly back and forth as much as possible.

The hardest part for me was telling Jordyn and Gabriela. Staying in LA seemed like such a selfish decision when it came to my friends. But they made it so much easier than I thought. We all cried, but they understood why I had to stay. I was sad to leave them, but I knew they were the kind of friends who would always be in my life no matter where I was, and the rest of my life wasn't in Pennsylvania anymore. It was time to go.

MY
SUPER-
GLAMOROUS
GROWN-UP
LIFE

When I was younger, I never thought that I'd move out of my parents' house a couple days before I turned seventeen. If you still live at home, and you think moving out sounds like a lot of freedom, you're one hundred percent right. I remember describing my first year in LA to my friends back home as a never-ending summer. But being on your own is not as glamorous as you think it's going to be, because with freedom also comes a lot of responsibility.

> I quickly realized that being on my own meant I had to be an adult even though I legally wasn't one.

One of the hardest things to learn how to do once I got to LA was setting my own schedule. It was hard to get in a rhythm of infinite freedom. Right now, my life is crazy-busy and free time just isn't really a thing anymore, but back then I had a lot of free time. But regardless of how busy or not I was, I always treated my videos like a job, because in the back of my mind I knew that YouTube was the only reason I got to be in LA. So it wasn't like I had nothing to do. I had my video schedule, an occasional collab shoot, or meeting, but the rest of my time was sort of my own.

I'm definitely a night person, and without anyone to tell me to go to bed I definitely had my nights where I stayed up way too late. Sometimes I would be working on videos, but other times I would just be going to get late-night food with my friends. One time, Lauren Elizabeth and I were texting back and forth at 1:00 a.m. about how hungry we were. We both lived in the same apartment complex but in different buildings, so it turned into us sending pictures of ourselves making our way down to our cars in the parking lot. We ate way too much breakfast food at Du-par's, this historic diner located in the Farmers Market at The Grove. And as you can probably guess, late-night adventures like this continued to happen. Which, in turn, caused me to sleep in, something I've always hated regardless of the fact that I'm a night person. I'm totally a workaholic; if I only get one thing done in a day, I low-key hate myself for being unproductive. I've never understood those people who could sleep until 3:00 p.m. When you get up at 3:00 p.m. the day is basically over. I mean, your first meal of the day is going to be dinner. I've just never liked the feeling of wasting a day.

At first I missed the structure of being in school. When you're a normal high school senior, your schedule is basically determined for you. You have to be up at the same time every day because you have to be there by the time the bell rings. Everything else you do, whether it's homework, soccer practice, an after-school job at Taco Bell—or, in my case, YouTube—happens between the time school gets out and the time you go to sleep. Because, no matter what, the next morning you have to get up, get dressed, and get your ass to first period.

But as a senior in online school living on my own, my life was super-free-form. My "classes" were prerecorded online lectures that I could watch at any time. And my "homework" was due whenever I felt like turning it in. The lessons were super-formulaic: watch this lecture, read these articles, take this quiz, write this essay, next chapter. At first I thought it was really cool; I imagined myself doing "school" in cool places like at the beach or on a plane. But I never did.

After a while, the lessons got kind of tedious, and I missed the simplicity of sitting in a classroom and having a teacher I could ask for help. And, as much as I hated normal high school, I actually missed having "class friends"—you know, the people you sit next to in class and joke around with but never talk to once you take one step out of the school. My new "class friends" were these weird animated students who would pop up after a lecture and have a fake casual discussion about what we learned that day. Animated friends are far less interesting than real ones.

As my days started to get busier, school just kind of fell off my radar. I figured I was pretty far ahead; I didn't have to worry about falling behind. But I did. And at that point my work schedule had ramped up because I was going on tour, so I had a ton of videos I needed to film in advance and it all just started to feel like too much. When I have a bunch of stuff to do, I stress out way more than I think is humanly normal. Instead of focusing on what I need to get done for the day, I tend to stress about what I need to get done in the upcoming month. So you know what I end up doing? Nothing. Literally nothing. It's like I know I have all this stuff to do, but I don't know where to start, so I just kind of shut down. I always get everything done on time, but it's such a stressful process that usually involves me freaking out on the phone with my mom at least once.

By the winter I got a call from the online school counselor (real person, not cartoon), and she told me I had to set a schedule. So I came up with a schedule where I did at least an hour of school every single day, and on days when I knew I would be shooting all day, or had a lot of meetings, I would do two hours the day before. Gradually, I learned to set a schedule for everything in my life. I write to-do lists for the day

May 2014

Monday	Tuesday	Wednesday	Thursday	Friday	Saturday/Sunday
			1 · Pack for UK trip · Edit and schedule upload main channel video — TEN THINGS GUYS HATE ABOUT GIRLS	**2** UK, Flight @ 5:45pm from LAX, Land May 3rd at 12:15pm	**3** UK · Film collab with Anthony AWKWARD ACCIDENTS / **4** UK · Digifest UK
5 UK · Film main channel video	**6** UK	**7** UK, Flight @ 10:35am from LHR, · Edit main channel video · Edit collab with Anthony, Land at 1:50pm	**8** · Film Main Channel Video and edit · Film gaming videos · Edit London vlog OCTODAD (EP 8)	**9** · Film 6/15, 5/31, 6/21 videos · Film TIO cutscenes · Edit London vlog	**10** *BEAMLY* WHAT I LEARNED, Edit & Schedule Upload Octodad 8, Mother's Day · Edit 5/24, 5/31, 6/21 videos
12 · Film gaming videos RESPOND TO EMAILS	**13** · Shoot Record Setters @ 11/12 · Shoot TIO Green screen (4) @ after · Edit Octodad/MCHG	**14** · Shoot Jenn and Andrea Show @ 12	**15** TIO LIES YOU TELL YOUR PARENTS SIMS 3 (EP 8)	**16** Film collab with Arden Arden and Lauren · Edit main channel vid · Iggy Azalea Concert	**17** REACTING TO FORM (scenes) / **18** · Photoshoot @ 3
19 · Shoot Jenn and Andrea Show @ 12 *8pm	**20** · Film 6/7 video (Beamly brand deal) OCTODAD (EP 9)	**21** · Film TIO Cutscenes (2)	**22** · ABC Family brand deal @ 9am	**23** Film TIO cutscenes (2) · Film 6/7 Beamly 6/15 · Edit 5/24 vid TIO CS (4)	**24** · Film TIO cutscenes (2) ACER CHALLENGE (vid) / **25** s-LAX @ 9:45
26 · Flight to Vancouver @ 9:45am	**27** TOUR: Vancouver	**28** TOUR: Seattle SIMS 3 (EP 9)	**29** TOUR: Portland TIO PRANKS IN SCHOOL	**30** TOUR: San Francisco	**31** ABC FAMILY BD

to help me not stress out about things so far in advance, and I have a crazy-large paper monthly planner where I physically write in everything I have to do. Vintage, I know.

When I decided to stay in LA, Andrea Russett and I had to find a new apartment. We had been subletting from UCLA students and the new school year was starting, so we had to get out. With very little searching, we found a place that seemed safe and nice, a large apartment complex mid-city. And by total coincidence, Arden Rose and Lauren also lived together in the same complex, which was an added bonus. We thought it'd be great; it was walking distance from The Grove, it had a pool and a gym, and it seemed really safe because it had a guard post at the entrance to the complex. But it's not so glamorous when every night you have a recurring nightmare that your apartment is going to completely collapse, crushing you and everyone else in the process.

Every appliance was broken. The dishwasher broke multiple times and flooded our entire kitchen. The oven smelled like gas whenever you turned it on, so we made a pact that we were never going to cook anything that required using it. We tried multiple times to have maintenance come to fix our appliances, but even after they came to "fix" them, the appliances were still broken. I think the worst was the broken air-conditioner. That fall in LA, there were record heat waves. Andrea and I would sit in our apartment sweating like crazy. The windows didn't have screens and when we'd open them all these bugs would fly in. We tried asking our apartment manager if he'd put screens in, and he said we'd have to pay for them ourselves. You'd think we would be able to cool off by the pool, but it turns out that in addition to paying rent, we had to pay extra to use the pool and it was pretty gross. It was so hot I would sit on the beach when I was working on my video ideas, not because it was fun, but because I actually needed the breeze. But it was also fun.

It doesn't stop there. Every morning a garbage truck woke us up way too early with its annoying beeping sounds. We lived on the eighth floor and while the elevators worked when we toured the building, conveniently after we moved in, they were always broken or under construction. We'd have to walk up

TOP 10 THINGS YOU DON'T LEARN, BUT NEED TO KNOW

🏠 Home   @ Tag   # Find

Jenn McAllister

1. WHEN YOU'RE SICK, NO ONE TAKES CARE OF YOU

When I got sick at home, my mom would pick up my medicine, make me soup, make sure I stayed hydrated, and even run a washcloth under cold water to put on my forehead. When you live on your own, no one does any of that for you. One morning during my first summer in LA I woke up sick. Like, really sick. When I walked to the kitchen, which was four feet from my bedroom, I literally thought I was going to pass out because I had such a high fever. Looking possibly the worst I have ever looked in public (very debatable), I went to CVS. And as I was driving over I thought, *I am sick, and I am operating a vehicle. This is probably monstrously unsafe.* Somehow I managed to get my meds, get home in once piece, drink water, and get soup delivered. But it sucked.

Jenn McAllister

2. APARTMENTS ARE NOT SELF-CLEANING

Because I shoot a lot of videos in my room, I like to keep it very tidy. Generally, I'm just a pretty neat person (except when I can't decide what to wear, then I will keep trying on outfits until everything I own is on my floor). But there is a difference between being "neat" and being "clean." When I was younger I helped out around the house. I did the dishes, took the trash out, kept my room tidy, even helped with the wash. But when it came to things like bathrooms, floors, and windows, I just took for granted that they were always clean. They are not. Our bathrooms were clean because my mom scrubbed the shit out of them. You have to clean stuff, even if it doesn't look dirty. Dirt accumulates; it's sneaky like that.

Jenn McAllister

3. GROCERY SHOPPING IS HARD

I know I sound like I'm joking, but grocery shopping is hard. After years of living off my mom's home cooking, I realized I basically only knew how to make sandwiches and mac and cheese. So the first time I walked into a grocery store by myself, I had no idea where to start. I ended up buying Goldfish, frozen foods, and soda, and basically lived on takeout for a month. (I regret nothing!) Eventually, I realized I was going to need to learn how to cook a few basic things. But even then I had to figure out how much to buy. Sometimes it wouldn't be enough, and I'd be back ordering takeout. Sometimes, I'd buy too much and have the pleasure of throwing out the moldiest food you have ever seen. Eventually, with some trial and error, I figured it out.

Jenn McAllister

4. HAVE A SPARE KEY

Once, Lauren and I went to a birthday party together and, since we went together, she didn't take her keys. But halfway through the party Lauren started to feel really sick and had to go home. So I gave her my key, put her in an Uber, and told her to leave the key in the potted plant outside our front door. When I got home later that night I saw the key, but it wasn't in the potted plant. It was on the floor of the entryway inside our house, just mocking me. I started looking around the yard and I found a ladder and prayed our balcony door was unlocked. The problem was, the ladder was just a little too short. We have these concrete planters around the front of our house, so I put the base of the ladder on the edge of the planter and it was just barely tall enough for me to climb up. Let me be clear: This was a terrible idea. This was basically like putting a ladder on a balance beam. Still, I took off my heels, threw them onto the balcony, and climbed up. But in order to get over the railing, I had to stand on the very top of the ladder. Did I mention there was a cactus in the planter under the ladder? So basically, I should be dead. I learned it's good to give a couple of your friends a set of spare keys, so you can call them in an emergency. Now if I'm locked out, I can just call a friend. I mean, I kind of have to . . . Our landlord revoked our ladder privileges.

Jenn McAllister

5. PLUMBING IS A RIGHT-NOW T

Especially after living in my old terrible apartment, moving into a house where everything seemed to work was awesome. The only problem I had was that my toilet sounded like running water all the time. I always thought about getting it fixed—eventually. Besides, Andrea's and Lauren's only flushed every other time, so I thought, *Score, I got the good toilet.* Then, one morning Andrea ran into my room when I was sleeping and woke me up by asking, "Um, can I look in your bathroom?" She opened the door and my entire bathroom was flooded, and the water had accumulated so much that it soaked through the floor, and the ceiling below, and dripped all over the kitchen. We had to get our whole ceiling replaced. Turns out plumbing problems are not a later thing. You can't just get to them when you feel like it. They are a right-freaking-now thing.

Jenn McAllister

6. HOW TO JUMP A CAR

There was a period in high school where my car wouldn't start unless we jumped it, so I learned how to jump-start a car in high school. Well, *learned* is a relative term. My mom showed me how to do it, but whenever it came time to actually do it, I'd let her take care of it. We got my car fixed, but my mom put jumper cables in my trunk when I moved to LA. So I've always had them and just sort of hoped I'd never need to use them. One day I was at Meghan Camarena's house and her friend Karla's car wouldn't start. Luckily, I had my jumper cables, but we were all so afraid to hook them up to the wrong thing and electrocute ourselves, so we Googled it. I am now prepared to jump any car at any time. Move over, AAA, Jenn McAllister's got this.

Jenn McAllister

7. HOW TO KILL BUGS

I've never been able to kill bugs. Once, in high school, I was home alone and I found a bug in my bathroom, so I just shut the door and stuffed towels in the crack so the bug would stay in there until my mom got home. When Andrea and I moved into our second apartment, our laundry room was in the basement. One day I walked in and saw a cockroach in the middle of the floor, and I got so scared I actually just froze until it decided to move out of my way. I was honestly standing there for a couple minutes. I know this is the part where I am supposed to tell you how to kill bugs, but the truth is, I still don't know.

Jenn McAllister

8. SET UP YOUR UTILITIES *WAAAAAY* IN ADVANCE

When Arden, Lauren, Andrea, and I moved into a house together in May of 2014, the gas was off in our apartment. Being the responsible adults we were pretending to be, we called the gas company and asked them to come turn on our gas. They told us they didn't have an appointment for five weeks. Now, I wasn't super-disappointed that we had to order takeout because we couldn't use our stove. But it turns out that our house has a gas water heater, so for five weeks we had to take cold showers. We finally gave up and just started showering at the gym—even when we weren't working out. So call your utilities in advance: Cold showers are terrible.

Jenn McAllister

9. YOU CAN NEVER HAVE TOO MANY ALARM CLOCKS

I have an unfailing ability to sleep through alarms. When I lived at home, I had my mom as a backup alarm. If I was late to school, the worst thing that ever happened to me was a 5:00 p.m. detention. But when you're in the real world, people expect you to be on time, especially if you're young and want people to take you seriously. So I've learned to set multiple alarms when I have to be somewhere early in the morning. While your roommates may think you're crazy when they hear three different alarms buzzing at the same time, it's better than your boss thinking you're a total flake.

Jenn McAllister

10. BUILD CREDIT

This one's super-boring but I think it's really important. Build credit as soon as you can. Having a good score is kind of like having a FastPass at Disneyland, or maybe it's more like getting into a VIP room, or, I don't know what it's like, but it's important and will make your life easier. When I moved to LA I made enough money to rent an apartment, but no one wanted to give me a credit card, let alone rent me an apartment, because I had no credit history. To the financial world, I was basically a ghost. I had to have my mom cosign for me. Which, though I love her, didn't feel awesome when the point was that I was supposed to be on my own.

seven flights of stairs. Sometimes with multiple bags of groceries. When they did work, the left elevator would drop a little around the second floor and then keep going up. The first time it happened I was so terrified, I remember thinking, *This is it; this is how I die.* But after riding up and down the elevator a couple times, it was entertaining to watch other people freak out when it dropped around the second floor. I hated that apartment. Everything was terrible, so terrible that in March of that year, my nightmare about the building collapsing almost came true.

When I first moved to LA, I actually wanted to experience an earthquake. It's like an LA rite of passage. Technically, I had experienced one on the East Coast, but because they are so rare back east, I didn't know what it was. At the time my mom was on the riding lawn mower and I was in my room listening to an EDM song when my closet door started shaking. I thought my music must be too loud, so I turned it down, but the room was still shaking. I ran outside and asked my mom if she hit the house with our lawn mower, and she looked at me like I was crazy. She didn't feel it at all. I found out it was an earthquake via Twitter, of course.

There were a few little ones when I moved into my first apartment in Westwood, but they didn't feel like "real earthquakes." Starting that fall there were all these predictions that California was due for a large earthquake, stories on the news that there would be heightened activity, and possibly even a really big one. I had my first real one in December of 2013. It was a 3.9 on the Richter scale, which apparently is classified as minor, but I didn't know that at the time, so I thought that was the big earthquake everyone was predicting.

Then in March of 2014, super-early in the morning, before the garbage truck had even started beeping, I was woken up by the loudest sound I've ever heard followed by my room shaking. I was half asleep, so my first thought when I was woken up was that my recurring dream was actually coming true. I remember lying in my bed with my eyes wide open, thinking, *Oh god, my dream is coming true. I'm going to die because I live in a shitty apartment complex.* We don't learn earthquake safety in school on the East Coast,

Jenn McAllister ✔
@jennxpenn

That earthquake just woke me up...

↩ ⇄ ★ ıı •••

so I had no idea what to do. And my building was so tall that even after the earthquake had stopped, my entire building was swaying from side to side. Surprisingly, my apartment complex didn't collapse, and I survived to tell the story (obviously). I read later that the epicenter of the quake was less than six miles from my apartment, which is why it felt so strong. But it was only a 4.4 on the Richter scale, which is classified as moderate.

We found out later that back in January of 2014, a local NBC station did a story on buildings in Los Angeles that were potentially vulnerable during an earthquake, based on a report made by the Pacific Earthquake Engineering Research Center at UC Berkeley. Guess whose apartment was featured in that news story? We couldn't be there anymore. There was so much wrong with our apartment and I felt so miserable living there. We were supposed to stay through August, but we decided we were going to break our lease in June when Lauren and Arden's lease was up and we were all going to look for a house together. A little older, a little wiser, and partially inspired by O2L, who were already living in a house together, we started looking for a new place to live. And this time we were going to be smart about it and make sure all the appliances worked . . . hopefully.

There are a lot of things you take for granted when you're living with your parents that you don't even realize you took for granted until you move out. You realize that things like condiments that have always been in your fridge don't just appear there, electricity isn't free, and that your roommate is not your

mother and doesn't want to do your wash or cook you dinner. There are a lot of things about being an adult that no one teaches you in school, like how to write a check or what to look for in an apartment. There are just some things that you have to learn on your own.

THE PERKS
OF
BEING
A
YOUTUBER

Being a successful YouTuber comes with a lot of perks. For starters, being a "professional" YouTuber means that you are your own boss and you can set your own hours. I've never really had a real job, besides one summer when I worked at an ice cream shop to earn money to purchase my mom's used car. And even then my bosses were my friend Julia's parents, who never really even hired me; they just sort of said I could come work there to earn money and I got to take home ice cream after every shift. It was basically the ideal summer job. They never really fired me, either. I think, technically, I still *work there*.

As a YouTuber, I've had so many incredible experiences.

When Bethany Mota, an extremely popular YouTube fashion and beauty guru, was a contestant on *Dancing with the Stars*, a bunch of my friends and I were able to go to the show as her guests. I've gotten the chance to be a social media correspondent for TV shows like *The X Factor* and *So You Think You Can Dance*. I also got to be a part of a video for an organization that helps motivate young artists, and acted in a young girl's script, which we shot at YouTube Space LA. In high school I was a total Taco Bell junkie, so it was super-cool when they invited me to a couple of their parties and sent me some gifts. Goldfish Puffs asked me to be their official correspondent for Z100's 2014 Jingle Ball, where I spotted tons of celebrities. I even got to attend the MTV Movie Awards, Teen Choice Awards, and VMAs, where I walked the red carpet with my friends. All of these opportunities were mind-blowing, but for me, by far the biggest perk is having the opportunity to travel.

Growing up, we didn't have a lot of money, so we never really took vacations. If we went anywhere, we had either saved up a lot of money for a nice trip, which happened, like, twice, or we'd just visit family. Before becoming a YouTuber, I'd only been on a plane a few times—mostly to visit my grandparents in Peoria,

Illinois. Peoria is no Chicago. It's just long stretches of flat farmland. I think the coolest thing I ever did there was either go to the local skate park or set up a Slip'N Slide in my grandparents' yard (though, admittedly, Slip'N Slides are ridiculously fun). In June of 2012, I actually took a trip to somewhere other than my grandparents' house: Los Angeles for VidCon. I remember thinking even the security line at the airport was exciting. I was probably the only person that the TSA had seen get excited over removing liquids from her backpack.

When I started getting more subscribers, suddenly I was flying to LA all the time. Once I moved out to LA, I got my first opportunity to tour: I was asked to be a part of DigiTour 2013. DigiTour is a tour of musicians and YouTube celebrities. DigiTour 2013 was a four-city October tour stopping in Chicago, Toronto, Philly, and New York that featured a couple different musicians, Andrea, O2L, Sawyer Hartman, a lot of British YouTubers, and me.

Each show basically worked the same way. Before the show, there was a meet-and-greet where we'd all sit behind this giant long table and fans would go down the line getting autographs and pictures from anyone they wanted. Afterward, all of the fans would gather in front of the stage and the show would start. Andrea and I acted kind of like the hosts and introduced different musical and comedy acts. We also did a Q&A on stage. One of the funniest segments was O2L's version of *Dancing with the Stars*; Andrea and I would get onstage and say, "We don't have celebrities, we don't have professional dancers, but we do have O2L!" Each of them would pick a partner from the audience, and they'd have ten seconds to put together a dance to a random song. I think Trevor had an unfair advantage because he's by far the best dancer out of the group (no offense, guys). At the end we'd all run onstage for a final dance party and some people would get in these human-sized hamster balls and crowd surf. (I never did it, because you only had two minutes' worth of air and the idea of suffocating in a giant hamster ball just sounds like a really bad way to go.)

We didn't have a lot of time to explore each city because we traveled by tour bus and were only in each city for about twelve hours; but traveling by bus was an awesome experience because we'd wake up in a new city every day. The front of the bus was like our living room/dining room/kitchen, with a speaker system for music, and a TV. Then there was a little hallway with a tiny bathroom, followed by a "bedroom" with twelve bunk beds. At first I was a little freaked out because I thought the beds looked like coffins, but I discovered that sleeping on a tour bus is actually, like, the best sleep you'll ever get. The movement of the bus is really soothing and the curtains kept the bunks pitch-black. The back of the bus was a lounge area with a wraparound couch and a TV, which we primarily used to watch the show *Sherlock*.

Going to Toronto for DigiTour was the first time in my life I had ever left the country, so before we left, I got my first passport. I was super-excited when I went to get my passport photo taken; I went to one of those photo places inside a Walgreens. I don't know if this is true, because some of my friends have much better pictures than me, but the guy there told me I couldn't smile, so my photo totally looks like a mug shot.

Because I was under eighteen, my mom had to give someone over twenty-one permission to act as my guardian or I couldn't leave the country. So, for a few days in 2013, Ricky Dillon was my dad. He had to show the papers at the border when we entered Canada to get me in the country. Sam Pottorff was also a minor, and he picked Jc Caylen to be his dad. That turned out to be a mistake because, while Jc is a great friend and would certainly be a fun dad, he wasn't necessarily the most responsible dad, and he lost Sam's papers. Sam had to spend another night in Chicago and fly into Toronto the next day when it got sorted out. My dad did not lose my papers. (Thanks, Ricky!)

DigiTour was such an awesome experience that almost immediately when I got back, I was itching to go on tour again. Luckily, just six months later, musician and YouTuber Tyler Ward gave me that opportunity. I met Tyler at VidCon 2013 really briefly by accident. Andrea Russett has a clothing line and we wanted to see her booth in the expo hall, so we snuck behind the curtain to try and check it out. When we peeked out from behind the curtain, we were standing in front of this screen. It turned out Tyler was filming a music video at VidCon, so we danced in front of the screen for thirty seconds and became a part of it. In April of 2014, Tyler asked me to come with him on his tour, the *Sincerely Yours* tour, as the host. I was super-excited to get another chance to travel, this time to sixteen cities, and meet more of my fans.

On April 30, 2014, I hit 1,000,000 subscribers. Sitting in my room thinking about those 1,000,000 people who watch my videos, those one million people who believe in me, those 1,000,000 people who make my life possible, I got so overwhelmed I literally burst into tears of joy. A lot of YouTubers do crazy things when they hit 1,000,000 subscribers. Jack and Finn Harries went bungee-jumping naked when they hit a 1,000,000 subscribers. Connor Franta went bungee-jumping, but, you know, fully clothed. A lot of people go skydiving. Arden Rose hired an artist to paint roses on her entire body. When I crossed the 900,000 mark in early April, I had started to I wonder if I should do something crazy, too. So when Tyler asked me to join his tour, I thought, *That's it. This tour's for a million.*

Say hey to your home for the next month!! We just left Denver! 👊 😬

Our tour started in Vancouver, Canada, on May 26. I was super-nervous because we had discussed how the tour was going to go, but we had never really rehearsed it. When we got to the venues, we decided to take a picture with the people who were first in line at every show and post them on Instagram. Before the show, I did a meet-and-greet that lasted a couple hours. During the show I would act like the host and warm up the crowd by pumping them up and talking a little bit about my experience in whatever city we were in, like in Toronto I would yell something like, "I just had Tim Hortons!" Then I'd introduce the opening act, a musician named Brynn, and tell fans to tweet me questions and I'd answer them when I came on stage again to introduce Tyler. Toward the end we'd have a dance contest where I would bring up one person from the audience and Tyler would bring up one person from the audience and we'd have a competition, kind of like the O2L guys did on DigiTour.

I was so nervous no one in the audience of the Vancouver show would know me, because the Vancouver venue was the only venue that was 18+, and most of my fans are 18–. I was right to be a little nervous, because I didn't have a ton of fans in the audience at that first show compared to the others, but it still went really well until the dance part. I normally pick a younger fan to dance with because I'm the worst dancer ever, so picking an adorable small child or someone who looked like they could maybe dance was the perfect way to win the dance contests. Tyler usually picked guys and together they would twerk onstage, which was hilarious, but an easy way to win for him. But at this show there were no young fans, so I picked this girl at random, and as soon as she got on stage I realized she was clearly drunk. We started to do the dance contest and when it was our turn, she pushed everybody back and tried to do a handstand and just completely ate shit. Handstands are not a cool dance move, especially if you are wearing a dress. (At least she was wearing underwear.) My dance partner in the next city was thankfully not drunk, or at the very least, she held her liquor really well for a fourteen-year-old.

After being on tour for that long, I quickly realized that life on the tour bus is a little less than rock-star glamorous. It's really difficult to shoot on the road. Even when we did get to stay in hotel rooms, I'd have to rig makeshift tripods using whatever was available (in one instance I actually propped my camera up on the Bible). You basically only eat junk food. There were no showers, which meant we either had to shower at an Anytime Fitness, which is a national gym franchise where members have access to the gym 24/7, or a greenroom. And, well, greenrooms are kind of like a box of chocolates; you never know what you're going to get. I remember this one greenroom that just looked like a lot of drugs had been done there. There was a bathtub in the middle of it and there were no windows, so it was super-dark. There was this weird

empty room at the center of it; you walked through the door and there was just an empty room the size of a small bedroom, with no furniture and a stained floor. While I can't be sure what that room was used for, if I had to guess, I would say murder. While there was a toilet on the bus, it had a single purpose. *One* purpose. If you needed to do any serious business you had to wait until you were off the bus and use a public restroom. I also got totally addicted to Red Bull. I started drinking Red Bull in the morning. And in the afternoon. And always. It got to a point where I had a headache if I hadn't had enough Red Bull. Our photographer, Kevin, was also addicted, so we would take these early morning walks to gas stations to restock. Basically, between that and the junk food, by the time the tour was over my body was, like, ninety percent chemicals. But the positives far outweighed the negatives, as each stop on the tour allowed me a chance to meet a new group of fans and to experience a new city.

Our last night was in Nashville, and we had a little going-away party at Tyler's bandmates' house and we all spent the night there. I was extremely sad to leave my tour family when the tour ended—we

TOP 10 HIGHLIGHTS FROM MY 2 TOURS

1. MEETING FANS (OBVIOUSLY)

My favorite part of the tours was honestly getting to do a meet-and-greet with fans in every city. For me, meeting fans is such a great and surreal feeling. I got scared in Montreal because security tried to shut down the meet-and-greet when so many more fans showed up than expected, and they wouldn't let me leave the venue. It was the first time I had been to Montreal, and I didn't want to let my fans down. After a lot of persuading, they decided it was okay and let me meet everyone. I have to give a special shout-out to the fans that came to meet me in Nashville. It was pouring rain that day and by the time I got to meet you guys, you were entirely soaked. It was an overwhelming feeling to meet fans with that level of dedication.

2. SIGHT-SEEING

Every place I went on tour gave me a chance to see things I'd only caught glimpses of on TV, in books, or on travel blogs. In Chicago, I saw Cloud Gate in Millennium Park (or the thing I knew as "that giant silver bean" until I looked up its actual name for this book). In Seattle, I had lunch with my mom at the top of the Space Needle, which rotates so you get an amazing view of the entire city. In Vancouver, we walked across the Capilano Suspension Bridge, which is this really cool pedestrian bridge that's almost five hundred feet long and hangs in the air over two hundred feet above this river. It was honestly terrifying.

3. BIKING AROUND CANADA

When we had some time in Toronto on the *Sincerely Yours* tour Kevin decided to buy some scrap bike parts from a thrift shop and build a bike. Yeah, he *built* a bike. He let me ride it around Toronto and Montreal. I feel like riding around those cities on a bike gave me a chance to explore them more than I could explore in other cities. In Toronto, I made a wrong turn back to the bus and got myself lost, but I was able to recognize my surroundings once I hit the coast and I found my way back on my own. Montreal was just so beautiful, and it really made me feel like I was in a different country because most of the street signs were in French. Unfortunately, we had to leave the bike in Montreal, but it was fun while it lasted.

4. PLAYING COOL VENUES

On tour I got to perform at some amazing venues. Philadelphia is the closest major city to my hometown of Holland, Pennsylvania, so it's where I'd go when I went to see concerts growing up. The venue that held DigiTour in Philly was the Electric Factory. Just the year before, Jordyn and I had gone there to see Ellie Goulding perform. The idea that I was going to perform on the same stage where my absolute favorite artist, Ellie Goulding, had performed was totally mind-blowing. On the *Sincerely Yours* tour in LA, we got to perform at Whisky A Go-Go, which is this super-famous concert venue in Los Angeles on the Sunset Strip, and our show in San Diego was inside this amazing old church that had been converted into a concert hall.

5. SEEING FAMILY

In Atlanta, my aunt, uncle, and two of my cousins who I don't see that often came to the show. It was a cool experience for me because they had never really seen me in my professional environment, and of course it was great to see them and get a chance to catch up.

6. TOUR JOKES

When you spend a lot of time with the same group of people in a confined space like a tour bus, you develop a lot of little inside jokes. On DigiTour, we got stir-crazy one day and decided to play a prank on Sam by hiding his tour bunk mattress and replacing it with trash. Obviously, we gave it back to him, but the look on his face when he saw that his bed had been replaced with old water bottles was hilarious. On the *Sincerely Yours* tour we basically had a secret language. Tyler has a habit of abbreviating everything. Eventually, we all started doing it. Ubers were "Ubs," the bus was just "the b," food was "f," and drink was "d." I feel like if anyone overheard our conversations, they would get a totally different idea of what "I need some d" meant.

7. ME TIME

This is going to sound super-dorky, but being on a tour for that long is hard if you're an introvert like me, because literally the only time you have to yourself is when you're taking a shower (and as I told you, the showers were not necessarily the luxurious kind where you'd want to hang out). So when we had a day off in Raleigh, North Carolina, because Tyler was filming a music video and everyone else went exploring, I stayed on the bus. I hear Raleigh is a great city, and someday I'll go back and explore, but I needed to be alone. I left the bus for a hot second to get my nails done, then I curled up on the couch and watched the entire second season of *Orange Is the New Black*. It was glorious.

8. GETTING MY TATTOO

For the longest time I had wanted a cross tattoo on the inside of my right ring finger. I would even draw it on my finger with a pen. I was raised believing in God. Whenever I'm having a terrible day and I go out in public to run an errand or something, without fail, a stranger will come up to me and say something nice. I see those small moments as little messages from God because after those small interactions, my day would immediately get a little better. My mom is not a fan of tattoos, so when I asked her if I could get a tattoo in high school she said, "No." When I told her I was going to get it when I turned eighteen she said, "No." When I told her what it was that I wanted and explained the significance she said, "I like it, but no." I finally just stopped asking. But gradually over time my mom would just start bringing it up in conversation. When I had a day off on tour with Tyler, my mom surprised me by taking me to get my tattoo, and I'm in love with it. Someday I plan to get the date I started on YouTube in roman numerals tattooed on my body somewhere.

9. PRETENDING TO BE IN *FULL HOUSE*

One of the stops on the *Sincerely Yours* tour was San Francisco. I was super-excited because I was obsessed with the nineties sitcom *Full House*, which takes place in San Francisco. I had seen every episode in syndication, and was totally obsessed with Uncle Jesse, aka John Stamos. While a lot of people might think of hippies or the tech industry, my images of San Francisco were entirely shaped by *Full House*, so I was just excited to see the row houses that looked like the house on the show. (I wanted to see the actual house from the show, but we didn't have time.)

10. HOME AGAIN

Even though I got to travel to see different parts of the world, and meet fans from all over the country, in some ways my favorite part of touring was going to Philly. Beyond getting to stand on the same stage where Ellie Goulding stood before, that stop on DigiTour was the first time Jordyn and Gabriela were going to see what my life was like and meet my YouTube friends. That night was really special to me, because almost everyone I loved was in one place. As I was leaving the Electric Factory I couldn't help but feel like, even though I was just a quick drive from home, I had really come a long way.

had gotten so close, and I wasn't sure when I was going to see any of them again. I think when you've been working on anything for a long time and it comes to an end, you feel a sort of a loss, but I think I was too tired to process it until I was on the plane back to LA the next day. About halfway through the flight it just hit me and I thought, *Holy crap, I just traveled across North America and met, like, a thousand of my fans.*

In addition to my two tours, I also got the opportunity to travel to Europe for the first time for DigiFest UK in London. When I found out I was going to London, I was so freaking excited. A couple of my friends and I extended our flights so we could stay after the show and really see the city. London was amazing. So many of the buildings have been there for so long that it has this sort of timeless quality. In the best possible way, it kinda looks exactly like you'd expect. There really are double-decker buses and vintage phone booths. The money there is so cool looking, except you have to be really careful because if you drop change on the ground in London you could be losing, like, five bucks. Also, in London they call the subway the Tube and we never got tired of making silly jokes about YouTubers on the Tube. For our last couple days in the city, we went sight-seeing and saw most of the touristy sights. We went to Buckingham Palace and Big Ben, and saw the London Eye. We even got a last-minute invite to see Miley Cyrus in concert at the O2 on the last night we were there, which was one of the best concerts I've ever been to. Even though we went to so many different places in London, I feel like we just scratched the surface. I'd always wanted to travel, but in this abstract way. Being there really showed me how much more I have yet to see in the world. I can't wait to go exploring.

A

FAN

SAVED

MY

LIFE

I absolutely love my fans. My fans are why I have the life I have. I know you always hear actors and musicians say things like "I love you guys, I wouldn't be here without you" to their fans, and I'm not saying that they don't mean it, but it's not necessarily true. Actors get paid by the studio to be in films, and while their fans have some bearing on the box office, ultimately it's studios that keep actors employed. And musicians do make money from tours and record sales, but ultimately all that filters through a record company. In YouTube's case it's literally true. YouTubers have a unique relationship with their fans in that, unlike traditional media, we really do get to live our lives because our fans watch our videos. My relationship with my fans is not something that I take for granted.

Even when I'm doing something as simple as buying eggs at the grocery store, I think, *My fans bought me these eggs.*

I feel like I have a special relationship with my fans because before I was a YouTuber, I was a fan just like them. I went to VidCon and waited in line at meet-and-greets to meet my favorite YouTubers, so I understand what it's like and how nerve-wracking it can be waiting to meet someone you look up to. Now I love doing my own meet-and-greets, because I like to put faces to the Twitter and YouTube names of the people I see supporting me online every day. I like hearing their stories. Some of my fans are also super-talented and send me really cool drawings. I keep all the letters and artwork from my fans in binders. I have a ton of stuff back home in my mom's house, but I also have a bunch of binders in my desk and even some in my car, so basically, my fans are with me in spirit wherever I go.

I arguably have the best fans in the world. I get so many tweets and DMs on Twitter that just make me crack up. Whenever I ask for suggestions for challenges or truth or dares, my fans always supply me with more

Dear Jenn,

September 2014

Aw jenn i love you so much! You've grown up so much AMARITE LADIES!!i7ii ♥♥♥ Your so inspiring and you make so many people happy :) including MeEE!! I love watching your fetus videos for my enjoyment omf. Your videos make me laugh so much loLz Your so fricken pretty, funny, inspirational, and an amazing person overall jenn! Your videos are so relatable too holy crap :) well ily jenn keep being you! ♡

Love You,
Haiwe

ideas than I could possibly use in a lifetime. There's no way I can ever truly have a bad day, because no matter what, there are always tons of people online supporting me. It's the best feeling in the world. My fans also know everything about me that I've ever posted online. When I first went to Canada for DigiTour, I tried Maltesers and mentioned how much I liked them, and when I came back on tour with Tyler Ward, my fans showed up with so many bags of Maltesers that now I'm sick of them.

By far the most memorable fan experience was when a fan literally saved my life. One time when I was working with a company called Fullscreen, Ricky Dillon, Jack Baran, and I got the opportunity to shoot a water stunt video on Lake Powell in Utah. The whole thing sounded amazing. I was going to spend a few nights on a three-story boat and get to experiment with different water stunts like Jet Skis, a human water catapult, and these water-powered rocket boots (which are boots that shoot water out of them to make you fly), and I was going to get to do it all with two of my best friends.

It might have been awesome, except for the fact that basically everything that could have possibly gone wrong did.

We flew into Salt Lake City, which seemed fine; I mean, it's the biggest city in Utah. Except that we (and, more important, whoever booked our flights) hadn't actually looked closely at a map of Utah. We had someone from Fullscreen named Jordan with us in case anything went wrong (and because none of us were old enough to rent a car), and he started entering the address into the GPS. We all figured we had a bit of a drive based on where we had seen lakes, but the GPS gave us an estimated arrival time of *six hours*. It turns out that, although there are a dozen or so lakes reasonably close to the Salt Lake City airport, none of them are Lake Powell. See, Salt Lake City is in northern Utah, and Lake Powell is half in Utah and half in Arizona—basically as far south as Utah goes.

None of us are really complainers and we figured, hey, road trips are fun. And that's when the real fun started—and in case it's not coming across in print, I am being extremely sarcastic right now. Jack and I both post our weekly videos on the weekend. We had already shot them and we had edited them on the plane, so all we had to do was upload them, which seemed easy enough. But it turns out when you're road-tripping through Utah, it's really hard to find WiFi. In fact, it's really hard to even find cell phone reception. But we figured, *A three-story boat where we were invited to make YouTube videos would have WiFi, right?* Wrong.

When we finally got to the lake, we found out a little speedboat was going to take us to the bigger three-story boat, and just as we pushed off shore, the guy driving the boat said, "Say your last good-bye, there's absolutely no reception on the lake." And just as those words came out of his mouth, I got my final text from my mom asking for the name and address of the hotel I was staying at. Now, my mom is the type of mom who worries. When my mom was still my "momager," I slept through a shoot once because I was so sick and she got so worried she called, like, six of my friends to make sure I was okay. When I can't get in touch with my mom, it's not good news. And little did she know, the place I was staying didn't have an address at all.

But my next thought was, *How am I going to post my video?* Now, I haven't missed a video deadline in, like, two years; I'm really serious about posting on schedule. But on top of that the video was a branded video, which meant on top of my personal commitment to my subscribers, I had a contract with an actual deadline and so did Jack. Jordan told us not to worry; he'd figure something out. At that point it was Thursday and we were supposed to stay till Sunday, but Jordan figured we had until Saturday to figure it out. He convinced the

TOP 10 MOST MEMORABLE FAN MOMENTS

1. MY PO BOX

When I opened my PO box in May of 2011, it was sort of a trend on YouTube to open fan mail in your videos. I had just started doing my *Ask Jenn* videos, and I wanted to have a segment where I opened letters, but I was nervous that no one would send me anything. When I announced my PO box I told my subscribers that I would mount all their letters on this medium-sized corkboard. The first time I opened the PO box I had enough letters and art to cover an entire wall of my bedroom. It was an overwhelmingly good feeling.

2. ADOPTING CHILDREN

During my Q&A at the Portland stop on the *Sincerely Yours* tour, one girl tweeted me, "Can you adopt me?" I thought it was the funniest thing ever, so I told Tyler and his band about it and they all thought I should "adopt her." So I did. I brought her up onstage, brought her backstage to meet everyone, took some pictures, and then returned her to her actual birth mother. For the rest of the tour it became a thing. At each show I would adopt someone and bring them backstage. People started calling me Mom, fans brought fake adoption papers for me to sign, and some even held up signs that said, "Adopt Me, Jenn!" I think I'm a pretty good mom; I follow all my children on Twitter.

3. FACE PUNCH

Like I said, when I was on tour with Tyler Ward we did a meet-and-greet before every show. I had never been to Vancouver before so I think my Canadian fans were especially excited to see me. One girl was so amped up she just kept saying something like, "I can't believe it's really you; I want you to punch me in the face." I told her I was real, but I did not punch her in the face.

4. SUBSCRIBE PILLOW

There's this company that's been making subscribe pillows since the subscribe button was yellow (now it's red). I always meant to buy one but I just never did. When I was on tour with Tyler, a fan gave me a subscribe pillow and I was so excited when she gave it to me. It's one of my favorite gifts I've received, and I keep it on my bed.

5. NOTES FROM LAUREN

A lot of my fans bring me food or candy when they meet me in person. When I was on tour with Tyler the whole crew was very appreciative of my fans because they basically provided us with enough chips and candy for the entire trip. We literally had a snack drawer stocked by meet-and-greet gifts. But one time a fan got a little creative; she wanted to do something funny, so she DMed Lauren Elizabeth and asked her for suggestions. Lauren told her to bring me mushrooms (because I hate mushrooms). So in New York City a fan brought me a container of mushrooms complete with a note from Lauren. THANKS, GIRL!

6. FOREIGN FANS

When we went to London for DigiFest, it was the first time a big group of American YouTubers had toured the city, so we knew it was going to be a big deal that we were there but we had no idea how big. One day a bunch of my friends and I went to this restaurant called Nandos for lunch. As we were eating, fans slowly started to gather outside the restaurant and wait for us to finish, and by the time we came out, we ended up having a four-hour-long meet-and-greet right there on the sidewalk. It didn't stop there—the fans followed us down the street and onto the Tube as we tried to travel to another part of the city and it was absolutely crazy.

7. LENS-BRACELET GIRL

Like I said, my fans remember everything I like. A lot of them will even call out other fans for not paying attention to details. I used to wear these bracelets a lot that looked like the outside of a camera lens and my fans noticed I wore them every day. One year somebody gave me one at Playlist Live, and then the next year she came back and brought me a second one. I recognized her right away. (If you're reading this, I apologize that I am the worst at names, but I remember seeing your lovely face and thinking, *Oh, cool! It's the lens-bracelet girl!*)

8. MORNING COFFEE

When we stopped in Atlanta on the *Sincerely Yours* tour, we parked the tour bus overnight a couple blocks away from the venue. When I woke up there were three or four girls outside the bus who had brought me my favorite drink from Starbucks. I was super-touched that they remembered what it was, and also super-excited that I didn't have to make a coffee run.

9. THE COSTA RICANS

I have these fans from Costa Rica, and I see them at Playlist every year. There's something nice about seeing the same faces coming back year after year. One of my favorite things to collect is money from other countries, and every time I see them they bring me a dollar from Costa Rica for my collection.

10. TORONTO GIRL

After the Toronto DigiFest show, we went behind the venue in the parking lot and there were a few fans waiting for us. We're not really supposed to hang out after a show because most venues don't allow it, but there were only a couple fans back there and everyone was being super-chill, so we hung out for a bit. One girl came up to me and told me she had been watching my videos since I started and she told me she was proud of me. She said it was so cool for her to watch me follow my dreams and have so much success. I almost started to cry; it was one of the nicest things anyone's ever said to me and it was so cool for me to meet a fan who had been there since the beginning. I saw her again on the *Sincerely Yours* tour in Montreal, and I was so happy.

company to let me turn in my video for approval on Saturday morning instead of Friday and bought us some time. He figured, worst-case scenario, we'd go ashore on Saturday and set up a hot spot on our phones or drive to a place with WiFi.

It was beautiful on the lake, and Thursday night, thinking Jordan was going to figure something out, we actually got to enjoy ourselves. Jack and I went paddleboarding at night through the canyon. Without the interference of city lights we could see every single tiny star. It was so beautiful. It was a moment I'll honestly never forget, one of those moments that you can't really explain or even capture in a picture. We all slept on the top floor of the boat that night. There were no walls, so we could see this beautiful scene of the lake from our makeshift beds and it was the perfect temperature outside: warm, but not too hot. It was kinda weird to not have

cell phone service. People say it can be peaceful to just turn your phone off and unplug, and I think it definitely would be if I didn't have a work deadline.

The next day we did all of the adventurous water sports for the video. The water rocket boots were definitely the best. It was a little hard to find my balance at first, but once I got up and stayed up, it was the coolest feeling in the world. The human catapult, on the other hand, was a terrible idea. A human water catapult is basically a giant marshmallow-shaped inflatable thing that floats in the water near the boat. Someone sits on one end of it and then someone else jumps from the top of the boat onto the marshmallow, flinging the sitting person in the air. I was terrified to do it and originally wasn't going to do it at all, but the crew on the boat assured me it was perfectly safe and I wouldn't get hurt. Again, wrong.

As I sat on the end of the marshmallow, I listened hard for the countdown, but there was too much noise between the wind and the sound of the Jet Skis surrounding the boats. I couldn't hear the countdown, so I wasn't ready at all. When one of the crew jumped on the marshmallow, my neck bent back so extremely fast and before I knew it I was up in the air. The wind had been knocked out of me and I literally gasped for breath. My back was in so much pain before I even hit the water that I think if I hadn't been wearing a life vest I might have drowned. I ended up getting whiplash and the pain in my neck and back stayed with me all the way back to Los Angeles. It may look fun on video, but it's aggressively not. Don't do it. Nobody ever do it. The crew admitted later that one of them had broken their collarbone on that thing a couple months earlier. Cool!

Once we finished trying all of the different water sports and the sun had started to set, we decided there was no real reason for us to be there anymore, especially since we needed to upload our videos, so we asked the owner of the smaller boat to take us ashore. We thought it wouldn't be a big deal because he was already making a trip to shore. The only problem—there was only enough room for half of us, so he'd have to make two trips. He refused. He said there was no WiFi within hours of us and it was his boat and he wasn't making more than one trip. He was selling his boat and he didn't want to put any extra mileage on it. And then, I don't remember exactly how it happened, but I started to completely freak out. Now, I'm not a diva; I'm not a complainer, really; I'm not even particularly outspoken, but I was in pain, I needed to upload my video, I had no cell phone reception, and I was trapped on this boat in the middle of nowhere. I had a panic attack and I don't remember exactly what I said, but Jack told me I had a meltdown and just kept repeating, "I need to get off this boat." I walked away and calmed myself down, but we still had no idea how we were going to get off this boat.

Jordan had told me he would figure something out, but he was at a loss. Then Ricky made a joke:

Wouldn't it be crazy if one of these boats around here had fans on it that could help us?

And without any better options, Jordan decided to give it a shot. He hopped on a Jet Ski and rode until he saw a boat with a family and a couple of teenagers. He asked them if they knew who we were and luckily, they did. So thanks to my amazing fans and their amazing parents who offered to take us to shore, we got off of the boat.

When we got to shore, there was a little motel with a restaurant attached and guess what they had? WiFi. We got our videos uploaded and I finally called my mom, who was more upset than I was that I had been put in that situation than anything else. We decided to start driving back up to Salt Lake City. We knew we wouldn't make it all the way there because it was late and it was a long trip, so we decided to stop in a town about halfway. The first town we found was kind of off the map, and looked completely deserted. There were a bunch of little restaurants on a single street but all the lights were out. There were no people on the streets. And then suddenly cars appeared, surrounded us on all sides, and came to a stop. Not wanting to end up living out our own horror film, we got the hell out of that creepy town and kept driving until we hit Provo, Utah. We got a regular-sized hotel room, but the clerk at the front desk thought we looked tired, so she upgraded us to a master suite with no extra cost. The next day as we lay out by the pool, relaxing, we were finally able to reflect and laugh about everything that happened. I don't regret going on that trip; it was definitely an experience I'll never forget. But seriously, without that fan, we might all still be marooned on that boat.

SHUTTER 180.0   EI 800   WB 320

76

THE
BEST
BAD
NIGHT

CLIP A001 C010

SxS 1 12

● REC

BAT 2 27.2V

I started making videos before I knew YouTube was a thing, so becoming a YouTuber was not my original goal. When I was setting up comedy shows with SpongeBob SquarePants jokes in my living room, I wasn't thinking, *I want to be a YouTuber*; I was thinking, *I want to be an actor*. Even after I discovered YouTube, I was never like, "Never mind, I'm a YouTuber." I still wanted to act, but at that time I just never thought I would get the opportunity. Then one day Lauren Elizabeth was like, "Hey, want to star in a movie with me?" Obviously my answer was yes.

The entertainment industry is sort of scrambling to capture our generation's attention. Social media celebrities aren't really taken seriously by people in the industry, but they pull in a lot of attention that traditional media just doesn't seem to get as much of anymore. They just don't really get it. They don't really get YouTube. However, this company called GRB Entertainment, best known for reality shows, does. They decided they wanted to create a movie around YouTubers, and they chose Lauren. They wanted to get another YouTuber involved in the project as well, so they asked her, "Who do you want to work with?" And since Lauren and I are so ridiculously bonded that she once got fake-upset when I went downstairs to the kitchen without her, I think we all know who she said.

GRB Entertainment let us be involved in every step of the process, so not only did we act as the leading roles in our first movie, *Bad Night*, but we also helped produce it. Lauren and I and our managers from Big Frame (the management part of AwesomenessTV), Byron Austen Ashley and Rana Zand, also signed on as producers to help develop the project, along with AJ Tesler. The five of us sat down with the directors, Chris and Nick Riedell, and the writer, Daniel Kinno, and we all talked about what kind of movie we wanted to make.

Lauren and I knew exactly what kind of movie we wanted to make. We wanted to make a comedy. I've always admired funny women like Kristen Wiig, Tina Fey, and Jennifer Aniston (go watch the episode of *Friends* called "The One with the Fake Party" right now). Amy Poehler is basically my favorite person in the world. I watched her on *Saturday Night Live*, and *Parks and Recreation* is one of my favorite shows of all time. Lauren and I have the same sense of humor and love the same comedians and TV shows, so it wasn't hard for us to make this decision.

Fortunately, AJ, Daniel, Byron, Rana, and the Riedell brothers were all on the same page. We all wanted to make a comedy. We all agreed on a high school movie, but we also agreed we didn't want it to be a normal high school movie. We all talked a lot about movies we liked and Lauren and I talked about what we were like in high school. Everyone was really open and accepting of everyone else's ideas. Basically, this movie was the highest-budget collab I've ever made.

We originally went through a lot of ideas but eventually based the story off of two things that happened to me at my high school. I told everyone about how on the senior trip at my school (which I never actually went on) they put duct tape on the outside of the hotel room doors so they could figure out who snuck out after hours. I also told them about my class field trip to the Met (Metropolitan Museum of Art) in my junior year, and how my friend Gabriela and I escaped the museum so we could wander around New York. We came back just in time for the bus to take us back to school, and my teacher and the other students never found out. We combined those two stories and used them as a starting point for Daniel, who brought in the action aspect.

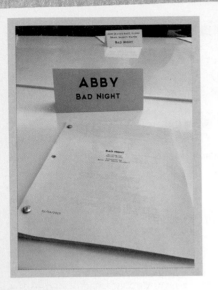

Daniel sent us, like, ten versions of the script, and after we read each one, he'd listen to our comments and criticism, and change the script accordingly. *Bad Night* is about (I would say "spoiler alert," but it came out two months ago) two high school students named Kate (Lauren) and Abby (me) on an AP Art History class trip to LACMA (the Los Angeles County Museum of Art). Afterward, the class stops at a shitty restaurant and everyone eats the disgusting-looking food, which results in them getting food poisoning, except for Kate and Abby. Consequently, the class has to stay overnight in a shitty motel. Kate and Abby decide to sneak out, accidentally get in the wrong car, and they have a pretty bad night. HA! See what I did there?

Both Lauren and I had done some acting in short sketches, but this was our first big thing. I mean, we were the leads in the movie, so we felt a lot of pressure. We both worked with acting coaches and learned how to create backstories for our characters, which we used to decide how they would react in different scenes. But besides all of that preparation, working with my best friend was the thing that made me the most comfortable. A week before we started shooting we had rehearsals. I was super-nervous because I didn't really know what to expect, but they ended up being really fun. It was just Lauren and me with the directors, who are the two nicest guys you will ever meet. We figured out how the scenes would play out together, tried them a couple different ways, changed some lines, and laughed a lot.

Before we knew it, we started shooting the movie.

We worked for months creating the concept and preparing, so when it finally came time to start, it felt like a dream.

Filming the movie was the best experience I could have possibly asked for. We were lucky enough to have such an amazing crew of people who were extremely nice and supportive of each other, which is apparently not too common. One day on set, Matt Walsh, who plays Ari and has also been in tons of other movies and TV shows, told me the crew for *Bad Night* was one of the nicest crews of people he's ever worked with. Having a crew that got along really well is especially important in comedy because it makes it easier for the actors to relax and just be funny. Definitely true—a lot of scenes in our movie are actually improv and everyone was comfortable to try the scenes different ways. June Diane Raphael, who is a hilarious writer and actor, played our teacher in the movie, and watching her on a set was like taking a graduate-school-level class in improv comedy. The camera would roll, and the most random jokes would just fall out of her mouth like it was no big deal, which I guess, for her, it isn't. I remember just staring at her like, *Whoa, I want to be that.*

Both Lauren and I became really close with the crew. On set, we spent a lot more time with the crew than with the other actors. Aside from Owen Smith, who plays Wheels, most of the other actors were only on set for a day or two. Like, you'd think I'd be close with Jim O'Heir, who played my dad (and also Jerry [Garry] on *Parks and Rec*), but he was only on set for a couple hours one day. We did have a solid forty-five-minute conversation, where I tried not to totally geek out that he was on one of my favorite TV shows, and we talked about YouTube because he didn't know much about it; he knew more about Vine. He's one of the nicest guys on the planet and most everything that comes out of his mouth is a hilarious joke. We became pretty close

with our hair and makeup people, Becca and Hannah; Janae, the costume designer who gave us our outfits; and the camera guys, Troy and Nico, because those were the people we spent the most time with. One of the PAs was actually from Bucks County, where I'm from. One day she took a picture of Lauren and me and texted it to me, and I saw that the area code from her cell was the same as mine. It was so random and also a great bonding moment.

We learned so much about how the movie-making process works from this whole experience. It was especially cool for me because I've always been interested in every aspect of filmmaking, so being a producer and getting the chance to be so involved was such a bonus. One of the things that interested me the most were all of the terms used on set. We obviously knew "action" and "cut" because everyone knows that, but we learned a lot more terms on set.

We had some insane moments on set. One of the craziest scenes to shoot was the scene where Abby and Kate find out everyone has food poisoning. In the movie, the class is on the bus about to head back home when suddenly everyone starts vomiting different chunky substances (in this case oatmeal or a mix of diced pineapple and mixed fruit juices), and Kate and Abby are so totally grossed out they are screaming "Help" out the window. In the context of the movie, it's far from the strangest thing that happens, but in real life we filmed this scene on a busy street in LA in the middle of the day, with other cars driving by and people walking down the street. When the cameras were rolling we were in character, but as soon as they stopped, I thought, *Oh my god, I'm screaming "Help" from an actual school bus with a bunch of kids vomiting and a crew of grown men filming me. Weirdest scenario ever.*

Another insane day on a set was the day I got shot. Okay, I didn't really get shot, but there's one scene in the movie where the bad guys are shooting at Abby and Kate in a skating rink and we have to take cover behind an arcade machine. In order to make it look real, they use these pellets with hard plastic shells that are specially designed so that VFX editors can make them look like real bullets later. Before we started shooting, the stunt supervisor told us that the pellets were totally harmless, but we didn't exactly feel safe because he was, well, kind of crazy. When the Riedell brothers asked him if he could show us how it worked, he just whipped out the gun and shot it at the wall without warning. Not exactly the reassurance we were looking for. And he totally lied; those hard plastic shells do actually hurt when they fall on your head (though probably not as much as actual bullets . . .).

The hardest scene to shoot was one where Abby and Kate blow up a car to destroy evidence. Even though it's the first scene in the movie, it's one of the last scenes we shot. Part of what made the scene difficult was that there was a lot of setup involved. The crew had to rig explosives that would actually explode the car without, you know, killing Lauren and me. We wore earplugs because we had to stand pretty close to the explosion. They assured us that it wasn't dangerous, but I was a little nervous, because most of the time when you're on set a lot of the crew is just off frame waiting for the next setup, but for this shot they were all a couple hundred feet away camping out in video village. But even though perhaps it should've been, that wasn't what made me the most nervous. Now, with most scenes in a movie, if you make a mistake you can just get another take. But we only had one car to blow up, so we only had one chance to get it right. In the end it all worked out. It turns out it's pretty easy to act like you're afraid you're going to die in an explosion, when you're, you know, actually kind of afraid you're going to die in an explosion.

Filming the last scene of the movie was a moment I'll never forget. It's a scene where we mix Diet Coke and Mentos to create an explosion and then run back and get into the car. And then it was just over. Usually the entire crew isn't standing by video village, a lot of them are off dealing with props, costumes, or equipment, or setting up at the next location, but for the last scene everyone was standing behind the monitor. I remember stepping out of the car and everyone cheering, followed by the entire cast and crew having, like, a twenty-minute period of hugs. It was so weird to film the final scene of the movie; it felt like it went by so fast. And the whole thing was just such an amazing experience it almost didn't feel real.

It still doesn't feel real.

TOP 10 WEIRD TERMS ON A MOVIE SET

1. T-1 OR T-2

Everyone on set communicates over radios or headsets because sometimes the base camp, where all the trailers are, has to be far away from the location where you're shooting. So if you're ever on a set and you hear a PA say someone's taking a T-1, it means he or she is peeing. I bet you can guess what T-2 means.

2. ROLLING, SPEEDING, CROSSING, STRIKING, SPRAYING

On set, people call out everything they're doing. Most of those terms were pretty easy to pick up from context clues, like in English class when you were trying to figure out what a word meant on a vocabulary test. When they say *rolling*, they literally mean they've started to roll film; when they say *speeding*, they literally mean the camera is up to speed; and when they say *crossing*, they're just crossing in front of the camera. *Striking* means they're turning a light on, and *spraying* means they're spraying hair spray in an actor's hair.

3. FLYING IN

When I first heard this term, I thought it meant someone was actually, you know, fresh off a plane or something. But all it means is that someone or something is running onto set. For example, we shot a lot of school scenes where I needed a backpack and I wouldn't always remember to bring mine to set. So someone from props would get the backpack and before they handed it to me they would say, "Flying in."

4. CLEAN SHOT VS. DIRTY SHOT

I know what you're thinking. A dirty shot has nothing to do with porn. Okay, maybe you weren't thinking that, but it doesn't. It just means that something else or someone else is in the foreground, usually because you're shooting over their shoulder (OTS). A clean shot is when only the actor you're meant to focus on is in the shot.

5. LAST LOOKS

When you hear the term *last looks*, it doesn't mean that it's the last time you're going to see someone, or even that it's the last time you're going to do that take. It's a signal for the crew to make sure everything looks right in the shot before they start filming. Continuity is really important in making a movie, so for example, if in the last take I had on lipstick but while they repositioned the camera I took a sip of water and some of the lipstick came off, the makeup artist would have to apply more. "Last looks" is the final check to make sure all that little stuff has been taken care of.

6. MOS

That acronym means that the scene is being shot without sound, usually because they are going to put music over it, like in a montage. But there is some debate about what it actually stands for. There isn't one letter in that acronym that everyone can agree on. Most people think that it stands for "mit out sound," and that it comes from the fact that a lot of old Hollywood directors were German and that's what it sounded like when they said "without sound." These scenes were really fun to shoot because you can say anything since no one is recording the sound.

7. VIDEO VILLAGE

Nope, it's not an actual village. Only one person on a set operates the camera, and it's not the director. Everyone else sits or stands behind a bunch of monitors with headsets to see what's being shot. The place where they do that is called "video village."

8. CHAMPAGNE ROLL

The hundredth roll of film used on any movie is called the *champagne roll*. Apparently, it's a long-standing tradition on a film set where they pop a bottle of champagne and everyone drinks a glass after the hundredth roll of film (well, except me, because I'm not twenty-one). I don't know how it started. But I remember seeing a bottle of champagne in the fridge on set, and asking, "Why do we just casually have champagne?"

9. THE MARTINI

This is not an actual drink. The martini is the last shot of the day. I guess because after the last shot, the crew can go drink martinis?

10. MOUSTACHE SUNDAYS

Okay, so this is not an actual film term. But on our last call sheet it said, "Don't forget. March 1st is Moustache Sunday, everybody should come to set wearing their best 'that's a wrap' moustache." And since so many of the other terms were new, I thought maybe this was also a thing; it's not. It was just a funny thing our crew did. Most of the people on set already had real moustaches, though, so it was a little anticlimactic.

But getting to share that experience with my best friend made it ten times cooler.

I think I live in a good time to be a female comedian. When *Bridesmaids* came out, I was so excited to see a movie that not only had a cast of ridiculously funny women, but was also written by women. I think a lot

of times, even when there is a female lead in a comedy, she doesn't really get to be the funny one. It usually ends up being the male lead, which leads to this stereotype of "women aren't funny," when I think what really happens is more like "women weren't given the chance to be funny." It's cool that we live in a time period where people are starting to get it. One of the reasons I like

my other favorite movie, *Seeking a Friend for the End of the World*, is that Keira Knightley gets to be funny. The movie is very dry and dark, but the relationship between the characters feels real and unexpected because they both seem like real and different people. It's not just like he's funny and she's just there, it's almost opposite. Even though Lauren and I do play the more normal characters in a world of crazy, we still get to be funny.

I never want to stop making YouTube videos, but doing this movie gave me the confidence that I can do greater things while sticking to my roots. While I made this movie, I also wrote this book, and kept up with my weekly schedule on YouTube. I definitely didn't sleep enough, but, hey, I'm nineteen, I'll survive. Recently, I've become obsessed with a hilarious show called *Broad City*, created by and starring the comedy duo Abbi Jacobson and Ilana Glazer, who took their YouTube web series and turned it into a TV show. The fact that such an amazing show started as a web series has inspired me in more ways than you know. Here's to the future!

WEIRDLY
SORT OF
FAMOUS

I really don't think of myself as being famous. Outside of YouTube events, I don't get recognized in public that often. But on some level, I have 2,000,000 people who watch my videos every week, so in a way I am, weirdly, sort of famous. When I signed up on YouTube in 2009, the website wasn't what it is now. When I first started, the most-subscribed user on YouTube had less than 1,000,000 subscribers. But what's even crazier than that is that even just a year ago, YouTube wasn't what it is now. It took me five years to build up 1,000,000 subscribers, and by the time you're reading my book, I'll have 2,000,000—one year later.

Events like Playlist and VidCon have changed dramatically. Now we can barely leave our hotel rooms without "causing a scene," and they give us security guards who usher us around like we're all the president or something. The only way I could walk around the floor at Playlist 2014 was in disguise. During one of my stage appearances, some fans threw Britney Spears and Beyoncé masks on stage. I really wanted to check out my merch table in the expo hall, because I had only ever seen pictures of one of my T-shirts, so I put on the Britney mask and Rebecca Black put on the Beyoncé mask and we snuck onto the floor. It was really funny because I tweeted all these random photos of me in mask, like me as Britney eating pizza, and me as Britney riding on the back of a golf cart, so a few fans knew it was me under the mask, but we successfully made it in and out of the expo hall without too much drama.

This year at Playlist Live 2015 was even crazier. It sucks a little bit because I liked that kind of casual interaction with fans. I tried to go to Starbucks the first morning I was in Orlando with Andrew Lowe to get a bit of that interaction, and fans completely mobbed the building. The employees were yelling for everyone who wasn't ordering a drink to leave, and it technically wasn't even the first day of the event. We didn't really get another chance to explore the hotel after that. My favorite part of the event was announcing my movie, *Bad Night*, with Lauren Elizabeth on the main stage. We didn't plan out everything we said, but we never really do when we go onstage together. We did a little improv to sort of build tension, and then they put the logo on the screen behind us and we made it rain with *Bad Night* stickers with our faces on them. The movie is something I'm really proud of and it was hard to keep it a secret for so long from my subscribers, especially when I post everything I do online and working on it was such a big part of my life before it was announced.

In these past few years, YouTube has gone from being a weird corner of the Internet for a bunch of weirdos like me, to a place where over 1,000,000,000 users watch videos every single day. But even just as a website, it has changed dramatically.

One of the most significant changes over the past couple of years is the way traditional media now interacts with new media. I remember when Andrea, Rebecca Black, Ricky Dillon, and I were invited to the MTV Video Music Awards to be social media correspondents. I think the idea was that if we tweeted we were

TOP 10 YOUTUBE THROWBACKS

1. STAR VS. THUMBS

Instead of the "thumbs-up" or "thumbs-down" YouTube has now, it used to have a star rating system where you could give a video anywhere from one to five stars. When the update first happened, there was a lot of backlash in the community because a lot of people felt stars were a more detailed rating system. It felt like YouTube was trying to be Facebook or something. The thumbs have really grown on me though. "Give this video a big thumbs-up" is literally a part of my outtro.

2. CHANNEL DESIGNS

You used to be able to customize everything about your channel, from clickable banners and font color, to the background. And even though looking back on them now, some of my channel designs were absolutely hideous, I still liked the ability to play with it. But on the flip side I think the way they're streamlined now probably helps new users build their channels, because everything looks at least a little familiar.

3. HOMEPAGE

I think my initial response to most changes on YouTube was "This is stupid," and then I'd get used to it. The homepage is not really one of those things because I thought it was awesome the moment I saw it. Google seriously knows us better than we know ourselves, so the homepage now is really tailored to each individual user. It has your subscriptions on one side, suggestions of what to watch, a list of videos you've recently watched, and more, which makes it easier to find what you really want to watch.

4. VIDEO RESPONSES

You used to be able to post video responses on YouTube, which was a really cool way for subscribers to interact with their favorite YouTubers. In so many of my early videos I tell people to make a video response (which is awkward now because it's no longer a thing), and subscribers would post their own videos inspired by my videos. People still make videos inspired by other videos, but having no video responses makes it harder to find them and sort of removes the direct interaction.

5. 40,000 SUBSCRIBERS USED TO BE A LOT

Like I said, the most-subscribed user in January of 2009 had less than 1,000,000 subscribers. The most-subscribed user now has over 35,000,000 as I am writing this sentence, but YouTube is growing so fast, by the time this book comes out who knows how many he'll have?

6. MESSAGES

YouTube used to have a way to private message other users. The button was in the top right corner of the screen and fans could message their favorite YouTubers directly, and unlike Twitter, there was no character limit (or at least not one I ever reached). Then they moved it to another place, which made it harder to find, and now I don't know if it's even still a thing but I don't think it is. If it exists still, will someone please tell me where to find it?

7. SIDEBAR BARS AND YELLOW BUTTONS

Basically, instead of a "downbar," YouTube used to have a "sidebar." And instead of a red subscribe button, it used to be a yellow subscribe button. In, like, a larger sense, these aren't in any way big deals. But in a smaller, much pettier sense, a lot of YouTubers just feel silly because in our old videos we reference sidebars, and a lot of people used to end their videos saying, "Don't forget to click that yellow button!" So if you're watching a really old YouTube video and you hear that, whomever you're watching is not colorblind or directionally challenged.

8. APPLYING FOR PARTNERSHIP

Back when I started, you had to apply to be a partner, and you had to have a certain number of subscribers and a certain number of views. You had to have a couple thousand subscribers, at least a hundred thousand views, and you had to be on good terms with YouTube, meaning you couldn't have any strikes. I didn't apply for the first time until I had 40,000 subscribers, but when I did, I got accepted. Now anyone can be a YouTube partner. You could make a channel right this second and be a partner. I think it's a good thing because it makes it easier for people just starting out to build their channels.

9. SUPPORT THIS CHANNEL

Now YouTubers have the option of adding a "support this channel" button to get donations to their channel directly from subscribers. I always joke that if I had every single one of my subscribers give me just one dollar, I would have two million dollars. Now, I would never ask that in a million years, of course, but it's weird to think that that's a thing that can happen. I think it's cool for channels that are just starting out and need money for equipment. Or maybe for people who are making short films and need money for a crew or VFX, but if you're a vlogger like me with my subscriber level and you have that blue button, no respect. Yes, I'm throwing shade. You are in no danger of going hungry, and you can definitely afford a new tripod. You don't need any donations.

10. YOUTUBE AWARDS

YouTube used to give out awards for things like "most viewed channel" or "most viewed video." They even had subcategories like "most viewed in the US" or "most viewed—comedy." They were just little awards that didn't really mean anything, but it was always exciting to get one. MyCollab got a lot of awards, and my channel got a couple. I remember I once changed my channel's country to the Czech Republic for, like, a week and I got a bunch of Czech Republic awards. But it was kind of cheating the system, so I changed it back.

there, we'd help draw in a younger audience. But they didn't really give us a chance to prove ourselves. They made us walk the red carpet in a group, which didn't really make sense because we had no real correlation with one another besides the fact we were friends. We only got interviewed by a couple people, and one person who interviewed us clearly only knew who Rebecca was because of "Friday," which was at that point over three years old. He asked her a bunch of questions about the outdated song and then just sort of awkwardly turned to us and asked, "And what are you guys working on?" It was such a cool experience to walk the carpet and see the show, but we could all tell that nobody really took us too seriously.

YouTubers were often referred to (well, really are still referred to) as the most famous people you've never heard of. My first cover was for a business magazine called *Adweek*. They were doing an article on AwesomenessTV and the article was pretty much "these people are super-famous but you've probably never heard of them." They did our makeup and hair and tried to get us to blow bubbles with our gum, but I was physically incapable of blowing a bubble, so the cover is Teala Dunn and Lia Marie Johnson blowing perfect bubbles while I just sort of laugh in the middle. I've since taught myself to blow bubbles; I got addicted to it for a while, to the point where I would annoy myself with popping my gum. But it was still cool that we got to be on a cover.

Traditional media is behind on the YouTube trends but they're definitely catching up. Some companies are definitely more open to YouTubers than others. I went to this event where *Tiger Beat* took a bunch of pictures of me and had me fill out a questionnaire that they pull things from to randomly put in their magazine. They also pull photos from other places, so I never really know when I'm going to be in it, but I get tweets from subscribers all the time and then I'll run out and buy the magazine. (Although sometimes I feel a little weird being nineteen and buying *Tiger Beat*; thankfully, I still look like I'm thirteen.) I still think it's cool every single time; I'm not sure if it'll ever get old to me. One of the craziest things was being featured in *Variety*'s 2014 Youth Impact Report next to actual well-known young actors and musicians. Shane Dawson and Jenna Marbles were on the cover of the *Variety* issue, labeled as "Rising Stars," and I think it was a pretty big feat for not only them, but the entire YouTube community.

Just looking at changes in my career over the past couple of years, you can see the reach of YouTubers expanding. In the summer of 2013, AwesomenessTV debuted a sketch comedy show on Nickelodeon that features some of my *Jennxpenn's Top 10's*, giving a whole new generation the opportunity to see my videos for the first time, but on TV instead of YouTube. Being on Nickelodeon is so surreal; I watched it all the time growing up, and seeing my face on TV is always so exciting. In 2014, JoJo Wright aka "JoJo on the Radio" interviewed Jack Baran and me on KIIS FM, one of LA's most popular radio stations, which was really cool. He asked a bunch of random and hilarious questions, and it was such a weird but really cool experience talking into a microphone and hearing my own voice through headphones. It made me think a lot about the possibility of branching out and doing voice acting, a radio show, or even a podcast in the future. And in 2015 I starred in my first movie, *Bad Night* (also, I wrote this book).

One of the coolest moments for me, though, was the Teen Choice Awards in 2014. In 2013, there were only two categories for YouTubers—Web Star: Male and Web Star: Female. In 2014, they expanded the categories to include Web Star: Comedy, Web Star: Music, Web Star: Fashion/Beauty, Web Star: Gamer, and Web Collaboration. My friends and I still group chat, and I remember waking up one morning to a text from Andrea that she was nominated. When I texted her congratulations, she texted back saying I was, too. I was nominated in two categories—Web Star: Comedy and Web Collaboration for a video I made with Rebecca, Anthony Quintal, Jack Baran, and Andrew Lowe called "The Fab Five in Real Life." It was a big moment for me because I always watched the Teen Choice Awards growing up, and now I was nominated for two.

That day of the event was really fun, a bunch of my friends were either nominated or invited, and unlike the awkward day at the VMAs, people actually knew who we were. Andrea and I were styled by Whitney Eve, who let us keep the clothes afterward. Our network got us reservations to get our hair and makeup done, a limo ride to and from the event, and a reservation at a nice restaurant afterward. There were so many people on the red carpet that the fire marshal actually shut down the carpet for a while. We all went down the red carpet doing interviews, and I was on the preshow. I remember it was so crazy-hot that day and the carpet was outside, and my manager, Rana, kept blotting my face with tissues. I didn't win (though, for the record, I was up against O2L for Web Star: Comedy. Six boys vs. one girl; I think you get my point) but I love them and I was so happy for them, knowing how hard they work.

As much as it was a big moment for me, it was also a big moment for YouTube as a whole because we were being recognized for being as diverse as TV and film.

The reality is that more millennials watch YouTube regularly than they watch movies or TV, and for the first time it seemed like someone understood that.

MY LIFE
IN
VIDEOS

I have a terrible memory, and I mean *terrible*. I get it from my mom; I could say something to her on the phone in conversation and, like, ten minutes later she'll ask me about the exact thing I just told her. I feel like my life has gotten so jam-packed that sometimes I'll forget smaller things that might not even be that small. I get the details wrong. But I know there are also some things that I don't remember well because I don't want to. I block things out that were too painful, things I just really wish never happened. There are definitely a ton of moments I remember very clearly, but when I was writing this book I had to scroll back through my Instagram and Twitter, dig into my iPhoto, and even rewatch my vlogs and videos to put the puzzle pieces of my life in the right place. Makes me wonder how bad my memory will be when I'm old and gray.

One of the things I love about being a YouTuber is I'll have most of my life on video forever. I know when I get older it'll be awesome to have this much of my life at my disposal even if I sometimes cringe at images of my younger self. Nothing on the Internet really ever goes away. When I first moved out to LA, I thought I accidentally deleted all my pictures on my iPhone. I created a backup, but the file corrupted for some reason, and I was almost positive I lost everything. And then I found this folder on my computer. It's filled with

thousands of files of every picture I took on my phone *and* every picture that I've ever sent to someone or that someone's ever sent to me. It's funny because I can't tell what the file is going to be before I open it, so sometimes a giant picture of Ricky Dillon's face will pop up on my computer. And regardless of whether or not I posted something and then "deleted" it, one quick trip to this website called Wayback Machine, which is an Internet archive, shows everything as it was on the date it was archived.

Even if it was deleted. So just remember that, kids, the next time you think about taking naked pictures or something. Don't do it.

My videos are basically a time capsule of my life, which can be kind of awkward and sad at the same time. It's weird to look back on friendships that are no longer a thing. I think when you lose a friend or when you go through a breakup it's a little like mourning the death of a person, in a sense. The person that you knew is no longer there anymore, because you don't think of them in the same way, nor do you have the same relationship you once had with them. Even if you date someone and you end up being friends with them, it's still not the same because they have a different role in your life. It's sometimes sad to look at old videos I shot with my old friends when later they betrayed me. But for the most part I can look at old videos and read old texts or tweets and smile. My videos allow me to remember them as they were in that moment and be grateful for the time we had together and the positive things they brought to my life for a while.

I often think about what it's going to be like once I have kids and they see everything I've done on the Internet. My kids are going to know exactly what I was like as a teenager and a young adult before I had them, and that's a weird concept to me. I've always been fascinated by my parents' old pictures and yearbooks, even though they hardly have any pictures because technology was far less advanced. There's just something about seeing your parents young that makes you think about them like real humans. When you're younger, your parents are just your parents. They often put their life aside to focus on yours and it's sometimes hard to remember that. I don't think I really started to think of my parents as real humans until after they got divorced and I saw my mom cry a lot. I saw her cry when her father passed away, but I was a lot younger when that happened, and being older and capable of understanding the pain she was going through made me look at her

TOP 10 MOST MEMORABLE VIDEOS

1. *THE JENN & ANDREA SHOW*

When I was younger, I really wanted to be a reality star, like the Kardashians (don't judge me). If you want to be a reality star, that's great, but for me I don't really think that's what I ultimately wanted to be. My self-esteem was so low I had trouble saying, "I want to be an actress," and I thought reality TV would be an easier stepping-stone from YouTube, either as a host or a blonder, smaller-butted Kardashian. *The Jenn & Andrea Show* was important to me because it was like I got to cross that off my list and see that I was capable of more than I thought. It was the number-one show on AwesomenessTV for its entire run. Also, it was just really fun to shoot. A very tiny crew followed us around and we got super-close with them. We did a bunch of random stuff like go to the remains of a house in Pasadena that is supposedly haunted (Andrea's scared of ghosts; I'm not, so I messed with her pretty badly). We went go-karting, painted portraits of each other, and tried candy from other countries. But I think my favorite episode that we shot was when we learned how to surf. Oh, and we did an episode where we went to IKEA to buy furniture for our apartment, and since it was technically a show expense, AwesomenessTV paid for my bed frame. Thanks, guys.

2. "MANNEQUIN PRANK"

While this video is not my favorite prank video I've done overall, it's in my most memorable videos because it's the only time in my life where I almost got arrested. I had decided to do a "Mannequin Prank" where I went to a local department store and stood by a bunch of mannequins while wearing a morph suit, you know, the kind of body suit that covers you completely from head to toe. When people would walk by I would slightly move and then I wouldn't speak, so nobody knew what was going on. Now, I have to get release forms, so I got permission from everyone who was in the video and if we didn't get permission, we didn't use the footage. This one woman walked by and before we even had a chance to ask, she yelled out, "You're not allowed to use this footage!" Fine, we won't. But fifteen minutes later she came back with a mall cop. He basically said something along the lines of "You can't do this, blah blah, you didn't ask the store for permission, blah, you could give people heart attacks, blah blah blah." He told me I had to delete the footage and he threatened to arrest me. Obviously, I was scared they were going to arrest me for pulling a prank, but I was more worried about Jordyn. She had been my camerawoman as a total favor, and this was in May of junior year and she was going to be applying to colleges that fall. If she got arrested, she would have to disclose that information in the application process and I knew I couldn't live with myself if I was the reason Jordyn didn't get into college. But this was my job and I had to deliver footage by a certain deadline, so I couldn't delete the footage. Luckily, sometimes my brain works extremely fast. I know, surprising. I asked Jordyn to hand me the camera and I told them I would erase the footage, but instead I cleaned my sensor. For those of you who don't know what sensor cleaning is, there's a sensor inside a DSLR camera and the sensor is open to the air when you're changing the lens. You want to keep it covered as best as you can, but obviously sometimes dust gets in. Sensor cleaning heats up the sensor and clears the dust so there are no spots. So the cop watched over my shoulder as I cleaned my sensor and I turned around and proceeded to tell him I deleted the footage. Does this mean I lied to a cop? It doesn't count! In the end, all that happened was he escorted us out of the mall—while I was still in my purple morph suit. It was super-embarrassing, but I decided public embarrassment was probably better than a night in jail.

3. "FALLING IN PUBLIC"

The first prank video I ever did was called "Falling In Public." In March of my sophomore year, a bunch of my friends and I went to Target and pretended to fall down to see how people would react. Basically, we'd carry a bunch of items in our hands, like a large stack of paper towels or a bunch of beach balls, and then we'd fall so the items would scatter everywhere and we'd make a big scene. We'd take turns holding the camera so we could film people's reactions. Most people were really nice about it and would ask how we were and help us pick up the things we dropped. Other people just looked at us like we were crazy. One person literally just stepped over my friend's leg and kept walking. We had a blast that day, which made me want to make more prank videos. That video, and my "Ellen's Dance Dare" video, helped me get *Stranger Danger*, my show for Teen.com.

4. "SUMMER BUCKET LIST OF AWESOMENESS"

The first video I made for AwesomenessTV was called "Summer Bucket List of Awesomeness," and I was so excited and nervous about making a video for a company for the first time. I spent forever coming up with the different things on that list, and then a second eternity figuring out how I was going to pull them off. My friends and I had a paint fight and an intense water gun fight. I even jumped in a tub of whipped cream (actually, I lied, it was shaving cream, but that was just easier). Not only did I get to do a lot of ridiculous things, but it also showed me how good it felt to work hard on something and have it pay off.

5. "PLAYLIST LIVE 2013"

Playlist Live 2013 is still my favorite event I've ever gone to because it was the perfect middle ground of feeling like a professional, but also getting to walk around the convention center like a fan. Everything about that moment in my life just feels so perfect. It's funny; if you watch my vlogs from Playlist 2013, I just look like I'm goofing around with my friends the whole time. And don't get me wrong, I was. When I started to rewatch the vlog footage in editing, I got really sad because I missed my friends. At the same time, I was also overwhelmed with the feeling of oh-my-god-I-can't-believe-this-is-my-life. I picked sort of an emotional song for the video recapping my experience because I wanted my audience to understand the significance my first Playlist had for me. But most importantly, I wanted to thank them for getting me there, so I wrote at the end of my video, "Thank you for your continued support. It has changed my life in so many ways." And I really, really meant it. (I still do.)

6. "EMBARRASSING OLD VIDEOS"

Right before I moved to LA I filmed a video of me reacting to some of my old videos. I chose videos (on purpose) that were no longer on the Internet. One was a spoof of a Geico commercial, one was a spoof of the TV show *Intervention* where I pretended to be addicted to Twitter, one was about chipmunk soup (I have no real explanation for this), and another one was my first video on MyCollab. It was so uncomfortable watching my younger self with her high-pitched voice and giant mouthful of braces. But I wanted to do it, even though it was embarrassing to show those videos because I felt like, in a way, I was sort of saying good-bye to that part of me. Except for the MyCollab video, all of the videos were ones that I had set to "private" when kids made fun of me at school. It was cool to see how far I'd come both in terms of skill and in terms of being comfortable in my own skin. The only reason I don't make those videos public now is that they don't feel representative of me and if I did, they would be sent to subscriber inboxes, and I'm sure you don't want a ton of videos of my twelve-year-old self showing up in your subscription box.

7. "BE YOU"

This was my first serious video and obviously it meant a lot to me because it was the first time I revealed a bit of my story. The video was also one of my first branded videos, for Staples's philanthropic program "Staples for Students," which provides school supplies to underprivileged kids. My only guideline for the video was that it had to be about school, so I started to think about what I had to say and I decided to just talk about my experience of being a YouTuber in high school. I was nervous to post it, but it felt good to talk about my experiences with other people in case they can relate. (If you haven't noticed, that's kind of the theme of this book.)

8. "INSECURITIES"

When I first started on YouTube, negative comments hit me smack in the face. My insecurities were so close to the surface that I really struggled with every piece of hate thrown my way. I slowly learned to love myself for who I am and stopped taking everything said about me to heart. I know what's wrong with me (or at least what people think is wrong with me) and it's just not something I choose to focus on anymore. I made the video because I wanted people to know that when you say the things you're feeling out loud, it takes away their power, and that everyone has insecurities, even if you don't think they do.

9. "PRANK CALL CHALLENGE"

This was my actual favorite prank video. The idea was that you pick a scenario out of one cup and a number out of another. The number corresponds to what position that person holds in your contact list and the scenario is what you have to say to them over the phone. The video was really fun to do with my friends and also super-embarrassing. I mean, I had to ask someone out on a date . . . And he said yes, so I sort of had to go. But it was also one of my favorite videos because it was the first time Andrea, Arden, Lauren, and I all made a video together. At that point we had decided to find a house, but we weren't all living together yet. We decided we'd make one for each of our channels, and that video is now one of the most-viewed videos for all of us. It felt like an exciting look toward the future, just four girls who make videos moving into a house together.

10. "MY LETTER TO MY YOUNGER SELF"

Sometimes I have nights where I'm feeling extremely creative and I'll come up with a couple ideas. It was the end of the year, the beginning of the New Year, and I had thought about doing something along the lines of a reflection of my year on YouTube but it somehow turned into a reflection on a whole lot more than that. I started thinking about these things I wanted to tell my younger self. At the time I was only eighteen, but I felt like I grew up a lot since I was sixteen, considering my transition from high school to LA. So I wrote myself a letter. Originally, I didn't know how I was going to use this letter to create a video. I started off by recording me reading it on a microphone and then just took my camera out to find inspiration. My mom had sent me this cool brass lens that doesn't zoom, but it has a twist focus that moves the focus up and down the frame, which creates a great shallow depth of field. I decided to drive to Malibu; I drove into the mountains and to a couple beaches and just stopped and filmed when something caught my eye. I love that video because I got to say some things that younger me really needed to hear, even if it's a bit too late. Also, the way the video turned out reminds me a little of some of my older, more artistic videos, so in a way the style, while a little more mature, is a throwback to my younger self.

in a different light. You like to think of your parents as being the strongest people in the world, and in a sense they are, but in the end they are still just people. I thought about it a lot when I experienced my own heartbreak. I had these flashes back to my mom crying and it made me realize this was not just a divorce: My mom was in love with someone and it ended. That was a real thing and it happened to a real human. It wasn't something that only affected my life and it wasn't just the end of the world for me, it was all of those things and more for my mom. I like that my kids are going to be able to see me and my life as a teenager and understand that I'm a real human who went through all of the things they're going to go through, too.

Right before I started posting on YouTube, I vividly remember thinking, *I will get people to watch my videos.* It's not like I had any specific plans or ideas on how to make that happen; I just really believed it would happen. I remember when that book *The Secret* came out, about manifesting things in your life, my mom told me it was something I should read, so we listened to the audiobook on a road trip. While I didn't connect to some of the things it said (I've never been much of a vision board kind of person), I connected with the idea that if you're motivated and you really want something in your life and constantly think about how much you want it, you can make it happen. Although I totally thought taping a dollar on your ceiling above your bed so you see it every morning when you wake up was so unnecessary. If I ever walked into someone's room and saw a dollar taped to their ceiling I really don't know what I'd think.

When I joined MyCollab, people *did* start watching my videos. When I hit 100,000 I felt like I was at the top of the world. I had people send me videos holding up the number 100,000 or a heart and I made a montage to celebrate. At the end I said, "Thank you guys all so much for all the love and support. Thank you guys who have stuck with me through this YouTube journey. I can't describe the feeling. Two hundred videos, ten million views, one hundred thousand subs, three years." It was my first big milestone. Hitting milestones is kind of funny to me. Like, for some reason, hitting 99,999 subscribers isn't as exciting as hitting 100,000. But then you get that one more subscriber and you're like, "OH MY GOD!"

I literally watched myself hit 1,000,000 subscribers. I had around 999,000, so I did a follow-spree,

jennxpenn

Style: Acting

Joined: **January 15, 2009**
Last Sign In: **1 hour ago**
Videos Watched: **6,536**
Subscribers: **100**
Channel Views: **2,375**

DIRECTOR

1,000,000 subscribers
42,182,174 views

jennxpenn

Joined Jan 15, 2009

which means I followed everyone who tweeted #JennTo1M and the link to my channel. It took under thirty

minutes. I just sat at my computer following people and refreshing, watching my subscriber number climb. I was

living with Andrea at the time but she was out, so I was home alone, which, in a way, was kind of perfect. I had

a very real sense of *this is where it all started*: at home, by myself, on my computer. When I crossed the million

mark I was so extremely overjoyed. I know it sounds cheesy, but I cried.

But one of the biggest moments for me was when I was asked to be a part of YouTube Rewind 2014.

For those of you who don't know, YouTube Rewind is a video that YouTube makes at the end of each year

starring YouTubers and celebrities who have big YouTube channels. For the video, they mock popular memes

and jokes, and they set it all to a mashup of all the most popular songs of the year. I've always watched the

Rewinds since they first started making them, when I still lived in Pennsylvania. It was always fun to watch the

YouTubers I look up to, and it was always a little personal goal of mine to be in one of them one day. And last

year I got to do it. I'm in the video for literally one second at 2:59 if you want to see me (you can't blink). But it

was just such a great feeling to be recognized by YouTube as being big enough to be a part of it.

Wow. I guess this is the last paragraph of the last chapter. But before I say good-bye to all your beautiful

faces, if you're already a subscriber, I just want to say thank you so much for all of your constant love and support.

If you're not, thank you for picking up this book and reading it; I hope you gained something from my story and

want to check out my channel.

A

LETTER

TO MY

FUTURE

SELF

When I was in, like, fifth grade, my class had to write about what we thought our lives would be like when we were thirty. It was a more interesting way to set goals for what we wanted to do and what we wanted to be like in the future, rather than just writing bullet points or something. While I was going through some of my old stuff to put in this book, I found it. So, when I was ten, these were my thoughts about my future:

I wonder what my life will be like when I'm thirty? I can't be certain, but I could guess how my life might be. I will probably be a cinematographer or maybe an actress. I in my spare time I would take pictures and draw and paint—I love to express myself. I will probably be married and have kids. I hope to get married and have kids! If I am an actress, I will probably have a nice expensive house an and probably live in Hollywood. I don't really know where I would live and what kind of house I would have if I was filmmaker. Probably still a nice house. Between now and when I am 30, I will have gone to college, and probably travel a lot. I love to take vacations, especially to the beach or the mountains! Whatever my future will hold, I hope it is a good one.

It's really interesting and kind of funny to look back on that letter now. First let me start by saying, for those of you who have never been to LA, Hollywood is basically the grossest part. There are a bunch of nice houses in the Hollywood Hills, but Hollywood itself is dirty and full of traffic, homeless people, and adults in head-to-toe Spider-Man or Jack Sparrow costumes. So, it's not exactly the super-glamorous location I had imagined when I was younger. But also there were so many aspects of my life I couldn't have even imagined. When I wrote this letter, I had no idea YouTube even existed. I already liked making videos, but I didn't know there was a way that I could share my videos with the world. I certainly never imagined I would move to LA at sixteen, and I'm pretty sure I didn't think that I'd be starring in a movie at eighteen. Basically, I had a very conventional idea of what a good life looked like: go to college, get a job, buy a house, get married, have kids, and go on vacation. Don't get me wrong; those are all great things—there's just a lot more to being an adult that I couldn't have possibly understood back then, beyond the surface stuff of career and family. Since I recently reflected on my life by writing a letter to my younger self, I thought it would only be fitting to try the assignment again. Because no matter how much my life may change over the course of the next decade, there are some things I know now that my future self might find useful.

Dear Thirty-Year-Old Me,

Look how far you've come. Remember when you were fourteen and you thought you weren't good enough and even considered quitting YouTube? Aren't you glad you didn't? I hope you never forget how much YouTube changed your life for the better. I hope you remember it's your fans that got you here, they believed in you when you didn't even believe in yourself. You owe them.

Did you create and star in your own TV show? Did you star in a female-driven comedy movie? Have you written another book? Did your close personal friend, Amy Poehler, ask you to give her a lifetime achievement award? (Okay, that last one's a bit of a stretch.) If you've done all these things, congratulations. You've accomplished everything you've ever wanted to and more, but don't let your success prevent you from striving to do more. Continue to challenge yourself like you always have and there's no end to the possibilities that lie ahead.

If you've fallen short, don't worry about it. The important thing is that you're trying. Just remember you still have plenty of time: You're only thirty, and while that may have felt ancient when you were a teenager, by now you know it's really not. You have time. Besides, I'm sure by now modern medicine has figured out a way for you to live to at least a hundred, so you've still got fifty or sixty prime years left.

Don't forget—money, fame, and success are not synonyms for happiness. You started making videos because that's what you truly loved to do. You were never in this for the money, so make sure whatever projects you work on come from a place of love. Life is too short to do things you're not passionate about. Motivation builds from passion, and you are in control of your own happiness.

Keep working hard, but don't work so hard that you don't make time in your life for love. Stay focused on your goals, but allow room in your life for a relationship (only if he's worth it). If you find the right guy, he'll understand when you have to be on set until 2:00 a.m. or when you can't go out to dinner because you need to finish working. Also, please tell me you've figured out how to stop dating assholes.

If you're married, don't take him for granted. You picked him because he understands you and believes in you, not just because he looks like a young Johnny Depp. Although hopefully he understands you AND looks like a young Johnny Depp . . . There's nothing wrong with having the best of both worlds. Make sure he knows you believe in him, too. You're a team now. There are going to be times when you fight, there are going to be times when he drives you crazy, and there are going to be times when you are so incredibly right you can't even believe you are having that conversation. But remember, your goal isn't to win the argument; your goal is to work through it together. You can't win if you're playing against your own team.

Do you have kids? If you do, I hope you have more than one (or at least plans for another). Remember how badly you wanted a sibling when you were younger? You're lucky that you found friends who were like sisters and brothers to you, but give your kid a real one. As much as you love your mom, it was hard when it felt like she was your only family. You're a family-oriented person, even if you never got the chance to be one until now.

If you don't have kids yet, that's great, too. It means you still have a little more time and freedom. Are you bicoastal? You love the East Coast just as much if not more than the West Coast, so make sure you're spending time in both. Have you lived in Europe for a while? Have you traveled the world? There are so many places in the world you wanted to see; if you haven't seen them yet, it's time to go exploring. Get lost. Experience cultures where you're not one hundred percent comfortable; it'll help you understand the world.

If you never got the chance to go to college, that's okay. There are plenty of opportunities for you to learn things every single day (there are literally YouTube videos about everything). Stay connected. Stay involved. Read everything. Learn a second (or third) language. If you did go to college, remember that learning doesn't end when you leave the classroom.

Are you taking care of yourself? Both physically and mentally? It'd be really great if you could do a pull-up by now. Work out. Eat well. Be proud of your mind and your body.

Have you held on to your friends? It took you so long to surround yourself with the right people; don't let them fall out of your life. These are the people you wanted to grow old with. I know it's normal for relationships to change as you get older; people get busy and people lose touch. But even if you aren't texting them fifty-six times a day like you are now, at least show up for the big moments. They'll do the same for you.

Remember to stay grounded. No matter how big your life may be, don't forget where you came from. If you forget, call your mom; she'll remind you. She always does. Also, just call your mom. Even if it's for the seventh time today.

Are you still staying true to yourself? It took a while to figure out who you are; don't let yourself turn into something you're not. Keep Being Yourself. Keep Creating. Keep Inspiring. Keep Dreaming.

Jenn McAllister, better known as Jennxpenn to her fans, has gained notoriety over the last six years on YouTube and successfully translated her following into working with top brands like Brandy Melville, Old Navy, and Mattel. She served as the official Social Correspondent of Goldfish at the 2014 Jingle Ball, as well as hosted a North American tour for musician, Tyler Ward. In addition, she recently wrapped her first feature, *Bad Night*, in which she stars alongside Casey Wilson, Adam Pally, and Matt Walsh. Previously, she was nominated for a Teen Choice Award for "Best Web Star: Comedy" and she recently participated in an online PSA for Voter Registration Day for Ourtime.org, which was featured in *Vanity Fair*.

To my viewers: I can never thank you enough for changing my life. Thank you for supporting me from the very beginning and for seeing in me something that I once couldn't see in myself. I feel so blessed to receive the amount of love I do from all of you on a daily basis, and I truly hope this book helps you in the same way you've helped me.

To my editor, Marisa Polansky: Thank you for dealing with my many emails and phone calls, giving me all of the help I needed to complete this project, and cutting the number of times I wrote the word *literally* from 72 to 45 (that's still a lot, though).

To my entire professional team, especially my managers Rana and Andrew: Thank you for believing in me and in everything I wish to accomplish professionally. I don't know where I'd be without your guidance and encouragement.

To my YouTube family in LA: Thank you for being there for me during the biggest venture in my life thus far and for continuing to make me feel loved and at home, even 3,000 miles away. I seriously couldn't ask for a better group of friends and I couldn't have done any of this without you.

To my best friend, Lauren: Thank you for caring about me way too much, always listening to me, and sticking with me through every single up and down. You motivate and inspire me to be a better version of myself (and sometimes you're funny, but I'm funnier).

To my best friends back home, Jordyn and Gabriela: Thank you for being you. Thank you for standing by me when no one else did, for inspiring me constantly through everything you accomplish, and letting me follow my dreams. I'm so extremely lucky to have found lifelong friends like you.

To anyone who has ever inspired me: Thank you.